Fellow Journc

"As a memoir of an Associated Press correspondent, *El Salvador Could Be Like That* puts the reader on the ground as a witness to the unfolding of a civil war, and provides the political and historical background that surfaces the underlying factors that led to the conflict. It is both a memoir and a cautionary tale of the true costs of war as seen from the ground and in the lives of Salvadorans. Frazier evokes the sounds, sights and feelings of wartime El Salvador. Read for its compelling narrative, for its previously untold history of a war, and to support the role of on the ground journalism in our collective understanding of the world."
  –Juanita Darling, Ph.D., assistant professor of International Relations at San Francisco State University, veteran Latin American correspondent for the *Los Angeles Times*

"This is so much more than the best journalistic account of the war that enveloped El Salvador in the 1980s. It is an exciting, fast-paced adventure story; an insightful analysis of the way nations break apart; a disturbing look at the war correspondent's life; and above all, a poignant, deeply personal story about a great reporter's efforts to come to terms with what he has seen and experienced."
  –Stephen Kinzer, International Relations, Boston University, award-winning *New York Times* foreign correspondent, author of *Blood of Brothers: Life and War in Nicaragua* and other titles

"Joseph Frazier's book brings all his expertise, compassion and flair to the deeply compelling story of that hidden war which cost 75,000 lives. His eye is extraordinary. He sees through the fog and disinformation of both sides, sees the war's political complexity, and makes us feel its human cost. And he gets its ironies—Kurt Vonnegut and Joseph Heller are somewhere smiling upon this account."
  –Journalist and filmmaker Mary Jo McConahay, author of National Geographic Book of the Month, *Maya Roads: One Woman's Journey Among the People of the Rainforest*

El Salvador Could Be Like That

Joseph B. Frazier

Karina Library Press, 2012
Ojai, California

El Salvador Could Be Like That: A memoir of war, politics, and journalism from the front row of the last bloody conflict of the U.S.-Soviet Cold War

ISBN-13: 978-1-937902-05-6 (paperback)

Editor: Michael Lommel

Cover photos: See photo credits in book.

This book is dedicated to the reporters, photographers, and journalists I worked with as we tried to make sense out of the tragic times that came to define much of Central America, especially tiny, bludgeoned El Salvador, in the 1980s.

I have never known a finer, more dedicated group of friends and professionals. It remains a club with no honorary members, one in which some paid their dues with their lives. I was honored to work alongside them and remain saddened that I won't see their likes together again.

The wars that brought us together are forgotten now. So are the lessons they should have taught us. This book is a reminder of both.

Contents

Foreword i
Introduction: El Salvador, A Re-Edit v

Backstory 1
Page One 11
Paz Wore a Bullet 29
The Red Ghost, Miguel Marmol 45
Pro-Búsqueda 57
Cinquera: The War and Small Towns 73
La Libertad and Surfer Bob 85
Word Wars 93
Liberation Theology and the Assassination of
Archbishop Romero 107
Mission Impossible 123
The Economic War 137
The Peace Treaty 149
How Much to Forget? 155
El Salvador Today 173
Linda 199

Foreword

When I showed up in Central America for the *Washington Post* in the fall of 1982, the region had already become a coveted prize in the Cold War.

An unlikely prize it was: a half-dozen little countries, all with anemic economies and few resources, and most with turbulent histories and little political culture. Before the late 1970s, no one really paid much attention. American newspapers traditionally sent their Mexico correspondents down to Central America once or twice a year to see what, if anything, was happening. Even then, few paid attention to what they wrote from sleepy capitals with 100 percent humidity and such obscure names as Tegucigalpa.

But times had changed. The broad-based Sandinista movement had overthrown a U.S.-friendly dictator and taken over Nicaragua in 1979, aspiring to make it a second version of Fidel Castro's Cuba. East German advisers soon were tapping phones in Managua, the earthquake-devastated capital, and Libya sent frozen chickens to fill the revolution's bare pantry.

To sap the Sandinistas, Reagan's CIA sponsored a counter-revolutionary force from bases in Honduras, where the military's cooperation was for sale, cheap. First secretly, then surrounded by a P.R. crescendo, the "Contras" mounted hit and run attacks on remote villages in the northern Nicaragua mountains. The Sandinista army vowed to chase them down but there were too many back roads and inaccessible hillsides. The result was military stalemate. But the turmoil caused further economic devastation in an already prostrate country.

Next door, the Farabundo Martí National Liberation Front was fighting a nasty little guerrilla war, with Cuban and Sandinista help, in an attempt to turn El Salvador into something similar to Nicaragua. With U.S. trainers and cheerleaders, the Salvadoran military was trying to gradually add, at the urging of the United States, modern military counter-insurgency tactics to its existing policy of massacres as a way to smother the uprising.

Guatemala, whose own Marxist government had been overturned by the CIA in 1954, was ruled by white-skinned generals whose hands were dripping with Indian blood but who could be relied on to line up against Cuba. Despite pressure from the United States, little Costa Rica was trying to keep out of the ideological storm by refusing to pay for an army. And just to the south, Panama and its canal (and its drug-money banks) were under the sway of a pockmarked general who, suitably remunerated, played along with Washington until George H.W. Bush suddenly decided to remove him with a military invasion.

At first, I understood little of this violent Central American tableau, having spent most of my career in the Middle East. I arrived in the region after an intense summer covering the Israeli invasion of Lebanon. Yasser Arafat and Ariel Sharon, that I knew; but Augusto Sandino* and his Tom Mix cowboy hat? I recall vividly my first landing in Managua, in the dark of night, driving from the airport past rows of rickety clapboard shacks topped by corrugated tin roofs and dimly illuminated by gas lanterns. This, I thought, does not bode well for the next few years.

But I was to learn. Little things, such as the fact that the best steaks in the world were to be had at Los Ranchos,

---

* Augusto Sandino (1895-1934) galvanized regional anti-American sentiment that grew from U.S. military interventions in the 1920s and 1930s. His name is retained in the Sandinista National Liberation Front, which took power and set up a Marxist based government in Nicaragua in 1979.

an open-air restaurant only a few minutes' drive from those shacks on the airport road. Big things, such as the volatile mix of Marxism and long-repressed national pride that had inspired Castro in the 1950s and still animated Sandinistas and Farabundo Martí guerrillas in the 1980s. Practical things, such as the timetable of airlines flying up and down the Central American isthmus, often through terrifying thunderstorms that seemed to arise daily about dusk. And sad things, such as the ease with which Central American leaders seemed to sell their loyalties.

Most of my lessons came from people like Joe Frazier, who worked in the region long before I flew in and who remained long after I left. He belonged to a small corps of reporters who informed his dispatches with sustained knowledge gained over years of reporting and travels up and down Central America. In writing this book, Joe has called on that knowledge and his experience to lay out for us, and for history, an extraordinary decade in the isthmus, one that changed all of us whom it touched, and Joe was one of those.

Despite the miles of newspaper column written during the upheaval and U.S. involvement there, remarkably few books, and none quite like this one, record the war from the ground and unfold its causes and effects, macro and personal. In that, it is more than the tale of one tiny country, or of the last conflict between the Soviet Union and the U.S. It's a human-scale story that should be read and shared on the nature and costs of war, and the nature and costs of reporting it.

> Edward Cody, foreign correspondent
> for the *Washington Post*
> Paris, January 2013

Introduction: El Salvador, a Re-Edit

SOMEHOW IT SEEMED all too familiar, having been in Vietnam not all that long ago: walking down a rickety airline stairway to the tarmac in Managua in May of 1979, smothered in heat and humidity in yet another country at war with itself, one of which I knew little.

It could have been Danang 11 years earlier and all over again, and on a much smaller scale it somehow reminded me of it. But it was Managua, Nicaragua, my introduction to Central America and a full-tilt revolution that eventually toppled dictator Anastasio Somoza and set the scene for a Marxist-leaning government—and more than a decade of regional upheaval.

I had gotten a first early taste of Central America that afternoon on the flight down from Guatemala with the late AP writer Tom Wells.

The Carter administration, citing human-rights abuses under Somoza, had cut off military aid and Somoza, the treacherous old bastard, had been rattling his tin cup around the region—including in the like-minded military dictatorship of Guatemala—for guns and bullets ever since, hoping to put down the Sandinista revolution that toppled him that July.

Tom and I waited for the Lanica airliner to blow down the runway of Guatemala's international airport. On board were just the two of us and four guys with embossed leather Nicaraguan government briefcases who sat together, well away from us, and talked in low voices.

U.S. equipped Salvadoran government soldiers walk by a truck burned by guerrillas near Usulután on the coastal highway, early 1980s. Photo: Luis Romero.

Joseph Frazier

We overheard one flight attendant say to another, in effect, "We'll be using the long runway this afternoon, we're very heavy."

A modern passenger jet. Six passengers headed for weapons-starved Managua from Guatemala. Long runway. We're very heavy....We weren't carrying helium balloons.

The short flight took us over tiny El Salvador, then an unknown territory to me. Tom, who knew it quite well, looked down and said quietly, "That place is going to be next and it's going to be nasty."

He was right.

Over the next dozen years a vicious revolution, the last bloody gasp of the Cold War, claimed some 75,000 lives, displaced a fifth of El Salvador's already poor population, and reduced parts of the tiny country of then five million to a bloody cinder. Passions still run high and it may be years, decades, before a solid, impassionate, and full history of the conflict will be written.

This book is an effort in the meantime to peel away academia and officialdom from that sorry conflict and present it as it fell on the backs of the Salvadoran people, the ones who somehow never really mattered in many official eyes, from whatever country those official eyes might have peered.

These are snapshots, rather than a textbook account, of the underbelly of a largely forgotten war that has wound up on the scrapheap with other equally forgotten conflicts. It is a ground's-eye view of that war and of what it did to the peasants, the soldiers, the school kids, the union leaders, the shopkeepers, the fishermen and artisans, the parish priests—the everyday, unremarkable people who often wound up in unmarked graves and on the edit-room floor.[*]

---

[*] I tried to focus my work at the time on these "unremarkable" people with mixed success. The beasts on the distant desks in New York will and must be fed the statements of Col. Whoozis and Ambassador Puff.

Introduction: El Salvador, a Re-Edit

Why El Salvador?

El Salvador has had more than two decades to cool since its 1992 peace agreement, and absent the East-West issues that expanded the war there, it is today an afterthought in the United States. The Massachusetts-size nation reverted in many eyes to yet another banana republic located somewhere down south of Mexico.

But when it looked as if the rebels might win and gain back-to-back victories in what we had long assumed was our safe, obedient backyard, the U.S. embassy in El Salvador drew some of our top diplomatic talent.

The United States spent billions of dollars backing a string of governments trying to fend off a coalition of five ragtag rebel armies in the tiny country. At the peak of the fight only Israel and Egypt were getting more American military help. The Soviet bloc used the neighboring and newly leftist country of Nicaragua as a weapons conduit.

More lives were lost in El Salvador during the conflict than were lost by the United States in Vietnam, and the U.S. population is more than 60 times greater than El Salvador's. The duration of the wars was roughly equivalent. Governments don't have friends, they have interests, and our interests there generally were not El Salvador's, but rather countering the interests of others, cost what it may.

I didn't believe at the time, nor do I believe today, that Washington would have gone to the mat for El Salvador against the guerrillas if other ideologies hadn't targeted it. There were no interests beyond a comfortable regional status quo that we had enjoyed seemingly forever and were hell-bent on keeping.

Prewar El Salvador had no oil, offered limited strategic value, posed no threat, and generally was not a nuisance of the kind that would invite our attention.

Our support came and continued despite knowledge of blood-chilling human-rights abuses, most at the hands of the Salvadoran government, a military we supported, and widely tolerated (within the military and the government) right-wing death squads.

As it heated up the Reagan administration drew the line quickly after the Sandinistas' victory next door in Nicaragua.

Somoza was the third in his family to run the country in a Nicaraguan dynasty of more than 40 years. It was begun in the 1930s by his father, Anastasio Somoza García—of whom President Franklin Roosevelt supposedly said, in 1939, "he may be a son of a bitch, but he's *our* son of a bitch." The apple fell close to the tree.

When Somoza finally fled the country one predawn morning in July 1979 with his beloved pet parrots and much of Nicaragua's net worth, some predicted the beginning of the end of the "safe" military dictatorships that had long dominated Central America. That happened, but years later.

Ronald Reagan, who took office in 1981, expressed no doubt that El Salvador, already boiling, could be the next domino. At one point he told America that guerrilla troops in Central America were only a two-day drive from the Texas border—blatant hooey.

The conditions in El Salvador were all there. No doubt many of the discontented looked next door to Nicaragua and thought, "If they can pull it off, we can pull it off."

When nearly all of a massively impoverished class has no route out of poverty, there is a class problem that will not fix itself peacefully. Much of the largely agricultural country was in virtual serfdom and kept there by private militias and security forces that served the tiny landowning minority. It was the Salvadoran way. It was the oldest joke in El Salvador,

Introduction: El Salvador, a Re-Edit

and perhaps the most repeated: the military and government were making guerrillas faster than they could kill them. The military and oligarchy somehow never quite figured it out.

Challenges to the status quo in El Salvador had been met by violent repression, murder, and bogus elections that left no way out except through the top—and in El Salvador that's where it eventually blew.

Many saw armed revolution as a desperate, last, and only chance. It was a tough, grueling, uncertain life in which many left everything behind knowing that the odds of survival weren't wonderful and that the odds of being left to rot on a remote hillside were not insignificant. Pick a "war name" or maybe "they" would come after your family. You might never live to know. You had to believe in it and believe in it every inch of the way. You didn't matter. The cause did. Or go home.

Civilian dissent grew into armed revolutionary activity which was eventually run by the larval stages of the Farabundo Martí National Liberation Front, or FMLN, beginning in about 1979. There was little doubt as to what Washington, with its decades-long history of military intervention in Central America, would do.

Nor, on reflection, should there have been much doubt that thousands of Salvadorans would head to the hills to join the rebels, reacting to abuse, death, and hopelessness over the decades—in the corn and cotton fields, the coffee plantations, the universities and classrooms, the churches and union halls.

Maj. Robert Coates and the U.S. "Case Study" in El Salvador

A 1991 analysis by Marine Corps Maj. Robert Coates, a U.S. military advisor in El Salvador in 1986–87, called the American presence "a long and massive experiment by the

United States" using advisors and materiel instead of American troops. He called it a "case study" for future American wars.

But Coates questioned whether such a limited American role was advisable. And in a short time, the United States got much more directly involved in places such as Iraq, Afghanistan, Bosnia, and Somalia.

Coates wrote that "Our military school system must teach and study small wars. It is a wonder that we can wage massive campaigns successfully, yet have so much trouble dealing with insurgencies...

"Ultimately, the United States must deal with the war in El Salvador as it did with the war with Iraq. Small wars will have many other names but it still must be treated for what it is: war...

"The business as usual approach to small wars, as in El Salvador, leads to incoherent incremental band-aid fixes. If our national leadership will not commit our national resolve to winning the war in El Salvador as it did in Iraq, then we should stop experimenting with our advisors' lives and the lives of the indigent citizens."

Coates placed the failure of the government to overcome the rebels on a reliance on moribund tactics. We could see remnants of those from earlier conflicts.

If you took the pleasant drive up toward the Honduran border through the cool mountains there remained some of the bunkers from an ill-fated four-day border war between Honduras and El Salvador in 1969. The bunkers' almost-cute pointy roofs and exposure to attack invoke more Gilbert and Sullivan than modern military tactics. About 8,000 troops died.*

---

* By most analyses the Salvadorans got thumped; they brought their troops home in a victory parade anyway along the newly named "Boulevard of Heroes." The name remains. Some refer to the clash as the "football war" because the two countries' teams had just played each other for a World Cup appearance and emotions ran high. It likely would have been fought in any case.

Coates concluded that unlike the government, the FMLN adopted new tactics when it realized it could not win conventionally.

He said the draft pool for the government drew mostly on rural young men, who were used to harsh conditions, capable when well led, and eager to learn, but that that's pretty much where it stopped.

The officer corps, he concluded, "came mostly from its own academy, which has produced a generally corrupt, lazy leadership unwilling to share in the sacrifices of war, hurting the war effort."

He said officers had no incentive to do well and often were promoted with the rest of their graduating classes, or "tandas," regardless of ability or lack thereof. Careers were secure through the rank of colonel.

An officer's loyalty to members of his tanda often rivaled his loyalty to his country. Thus the military mirrored the divisions in the larger Salvadoran society.

It is hard to say exactly what the United States might have been prepared to do if it looked as if the FMLN were on the cusp of an outright military victory of the kind the Sandinistas scored against Somoza in Nicaragua in 1979.

Contingency plans must have been in place or at least on the table. The Reagan administration pulled no punches in its dislike of the Sandinistas, only in part because they were exporting their revolution, Sandinista denials aside.

An invasion of the tiny country to prop up the army seemed somehow unlikely given the home-grown nature of the revolution and the difficulty in determining who was who. Whom does one shoot?

A likely reaction in the event of a leftist military victory lay just north, in Honduras, from which the United States already was directing the Contra War against Nicaragua's Sandinista government. Honduras has remote, inhospitable borders with both countries, and that campaign could have been extended to El Salvador, probably quite easily. It never came to that.

We were flooding the place with materiel and training well before 1983, when dire predictions seemed to have peaked. We were firmly implanted in El Salvador, although without American combat forces.

American reach in El Salvador quietly went way beyond sending supplies and money. The term "proconsul" occasionally popped up to the intense displeasure of the U.S. Embassy.

In 1984 José Napoleón Duarte, the country's first freely elected and civilian president in half a century, famously complained that he wasn't in charge of his own country, Washington was.

In a 1984 *Playboy* interview he was asked if American military advisors told him how to run the war.

"This is the problem, no? The root of this problem is that the aid is given under such conditions that its use is really decided by the Americans and not by us.

"Decisions like how many planes or helicopters we buy, how we spend our money, how many we need, how many bullets of what caliber, how many pairs of boots...all of that. And all of that money is spent over there in the U.S....."

It appeared while he was out of the country. Upon his return he denied the remarks but said he had not read the *Playboy* story.

Washington downplayed some of the more horrific human-rights abuses and massacres in our hemisphere's recent history, hoping to buy time and prevent another guerrilla victory in

Central America; Thus a Congress that had had a bellyful of Salvadoran human-rights abuses was charmed into keeping the money flowing.

But El Salvador was too small to cover up all that went on, and in the villages, countryside, roadsides, parking lots, and empty fields the dead somehow never stopped turning up. A truth commission convened as part of the peace deal reported to the United Nations that the military and the civilian right were behind about 85 percent of it, and said it identified enough of a pattern to at least strongly suggest that mass murder at times was government policy.

The five rebel armies of the FMLN were far from squeaky-clean, but by far most of the civilian blood was on the hands of a government that could not or would not housebreak its military and security forces—or eliminate the death squads.

Reclaiming Peace, and My Own

I stumbled into this unhappy stew in the summer of 1979 after covering the Sandinista war in Nicaragua and before the American-backed Contra War aimed at driving them out got serious.

I covered El Salvador from 1979–1986, the worst of the war years, for The Associated Press—which has generously given me use of my stories for this project.

In addition to wartime coverage, I visited several times later for the AP, and after retirement took solo road trips down from Oregon in 2009 and 2011. I came away with the partial belief that the worst of times have eased.

Many younger Salvadorans know little of the recent war, and the country has joined other countries with skeletons in their closets in a debate around what the coming-of-age generations should know about what happened just down the street and not that long ago.

Spain is looking anew into horrors of the Franco years, the French are revising their treatment of the fate of the Jews there in World War II, dictators in South America are being belatedly brought to dock over outrages they committed, often decades after the fact.

As late as October of 2011, Argentina's Supreme Court gave a life sentence to Alfredo Astiz, then 59, for crimes against humanity during the 1976–1983 dictatorship, in which an estimated 30,000 so-called political prisoners died. Astiz carried the charming nickname "Blond Angel of Death."

Different cultures and different countries are dealing with these things in different ways long after the blood and tears have dried.

El Salvador passed a massive amnesty, which not everyone loves, in 1993. Barring its unlikely reversal, and because of statutes of limitations, it is unlikely many more Salvadorans will be called to account there for a long list of human rights abuses.

The country still wrestles with whether to kick dirt over what happened and move on, or to teach the recent past, hoping it will not be repeated. Many coming-of-age Salvadorans weren't born during the worst of times and are showing signs of a disconnect. This worries many who suffered through it.

Many former political prisoners, rebels, union leaders, churchmen, and others say now is the time to tell their stories to avoid a repeat of those years, and that they want their country to listen.

Conservatives' opposition to this is strong. Let's let it be, they say.

Introduction: El Salvador, a Re-Edit

Scores of violent events there will always be with me. Even more so the realization that after a few years the massacres, murders, and bombs in the night stopped making an impression—I began to assume death and suffering were nothing out of the ordinary. Much of the nation was subject to that same numbness. If you stew in violence long enough it ceases to shock or stun, and a piece of your soul dies with the war victims. That troubles me today as much as anything.

The lack of an East-West interest there should help El Salvador avoid being loved to death yet again by contending major powers.

In 1982 or 1983 some of us were relaxing on a black-sand beach near the capital at La Libertad (there were many long quiet spells) with the late Ricardo Stein, a Guatemalan scholar from the Jesuit-run University of Central America in San Salvador.

Dealing with the United States, he said, is like a roll in the hay with an elephant.

You get a tremendous amount of affection. You may get crushed. But you learn one whole hell of a lot about elephants.

El Salvador had its own issues, lots of them, but suffered even more as other, larger powers used the tiny place to slug out their own differences.

The FMLN rebels the Americans opposed so hard for years won control of the government in the 2009 elections, after 20 years of post-war rightist administrations. It is not the hard-core rebel force that drove the left during its larval years (and beyond, to a point). Think FMLN-Lite. The United States spent billions of dollars to defeat them, but has since increased its foreign aid to El Salvador—and thus indirectly to the FMLN.

I believe the journalists I worked with there in those years were among the finest anywhere. Too many of them died trying to get the story out.

Many of the living will stroke a graying whisker or two and say, "No, it wasn't that way at all, it was this way, or this." But these are my recollections.

Whether with time and absence of external pressures El Salvador could have mended its differences and avoided the horrible fate that befell it is an open question. My guess is that it would not have. By 1980 it was far beyond the talking stage; the hatreds and differences were too deep.

We'll never know.

Backstory

IN LINE AT a San Salvador grocery store in the fall of 1979, AP photographer Pat Hamilton and I waited next to a middle-aged American couple, probably retired and obviously residents in the tiny country on the cusp of a nasty 12-year civil war.

We exchanged the usual pleasantries—who were we, what brought us to El Salvador. "Isn't life lovely here?" they asked us. "Aren't the local people polite?"

When we explained our purpose, the tone hardened. "Yes, it's getting a little tense," the woman sniffed, adding something like, "If you people would just go back where you came from, the problems here would all go away."[*]

But El Salvador wasn't on the edge of revolution because of us. The problems went back at least a century. The pressures had only intensified in the past 50 years, leaving no vent but through the top. And by 1979 rebel forces had been forming and bodies had been showing up in the streets, outside union halls, and at peasant cooperatives for some time.

It was a story of too many people, not enough land, and a tiny land-owning elite very much set in its ways, bolstered by public and private police and security forces; of a justice system that seemed to exist in name only—and anyway wasn't for the benefit of just anybody; a parade of military

---

[*] We forbore to mention to our new acquaintances that the quaint practice the ancient Greeks had of beheading the bearers of bad news was no longer in vogue.

Undated picture of a demonstration in downtown San Salvador, circa 1979. The national cathedral is in the background. Such marches were fairly common at the time. Police sometimes opened fire on demonstrators. Photo: Pat Hamilton.

governments and rigged elections that generally removed the chance for peaceful change. And hunger. And infant mortality.

Then out of the blue on October 15, 1979, a coup engineered by two reform-minded colonels tossed out General and President Carlos Humberto Romero, leading to the establishment of a series of revolutionary juntas that enacted wide-ranging reforms—including nationalization of banks and key industries, the breakup of the largest land-holdings for redistribution, and other changes that infuriated the land-owning classes. Death-squad activity increased in reaction, and there appeared to be a lack of political will to include the left in any attempts to remake the government and society under terms either side would accept.

Back in Managua, a revolution had ended that year with a leftist win. A political cartoonist who signed his works in the Sandinista newspaper *Baricada* as "Roger," and whose work I admired greatly, had his own take on Salvadoran land reform. He drew a cartoon of the bullet-pocked skeletal remains of a Salvadoran peasant half in his grave as brass-hat military officers asked him, in effect, "See, aren't you happy now, you have your own plot of land."

Most of the Salvadoran tragedy has its roots in the story of land and who held it.

Nobody was happy, and leftist takeovers in Cuba and Nicaragua that toppled military dictators gave inspiration to the Salvadoran underclass and furrowed the brows of much of the oligarchy, who were sure they were immune.

I mean here? In El Salvador? Really?!

It did happen.

For years indigo (used to make blue dye) was the country's main cash crop until synthetics were developed and the industry wilted. Early indigo growers were attracted to the lands that grew it and left what they saw as useless old volcanic soil to the subsistence farmers—until it was discovered that those areas grew really great coffee.

The elite, which had controlled the legislature through seemingly endless constitutional revisions, was in a position to take over the land as demands for coffee grew.

In the colonial era Spain had been mostly supportive of the concept of communal Indian lands, which allowed subsistence farmers to feed their families, however basically.

After independence, however, private landholders, with the help of government decrees, began seizing those lands as coffee became a valuable export crop and replaced indigo farming.

The favored status of export-oriented crops was formalized by decree in 1879. Private landowners could take over title to common lands if they planted at least 25 percent of it with specific crops.

The *tierras comunales*, or communal Indian lands, were abolished in 1881. By the next year private property was the only legally recognized form of land ownership. The Indian farmers were reduced to sharecropper status or became squatters on newly privatized land.

Rapid population growth put pressure on what land there was, and the expansion of cotton farming removed huge tracts of land from subsistence farming.

Tensions naturally mounted as more and more land went to a handful of owners. By 1912 the government had formed the National Guard, using Spain's Guardia Civil as a model, to watch over coffee growers' interests in the face of rising demands by workers.*

---

* The National Guard, disbanded as part of the 1992 peace accords, piled up one of the more abysmal human-rights records of any of the Salvadoran military or security forces—no small accomplishment.

After a rare open presidential election in 1931, the winner, Arturo Arajuo, was bounced in a coup that December. He was replaced by one of the coup engineers: Gen. Maximiliano Hernández Martínez, Arajuo's vice president. The Martínez military government was recognized by the United States after the general agreed to hold elections—which he eventually did, with himself as the only candidate.* Around the time of the Martínez coup, events converged that would influence El Salvador's future for the next 60 years and eventually draw it into civil war.

To begin, the general established the military as the main power in the country and cemented the military-elite alliance that lasted half a century. In the very early 1930s the Communist Party of El Salvador was formed. In 1931 a young firebrand named Agustin Farabundo Martí, sent into exile ahead of the elections because of his communist leanings, returned from the United States, where had he spent time with American leftists, as well as President Herbert Hoover (hardly a bomb-throwing revolutionary).

In the late 1920s world coffee prices fell by half and the wages of the field workers, already low, were cut by at least that much. Increasingly the workers were drawn to Martí and the new Salvadoran Communist Party.

---

* Military governments continued until 1979. Gen. Hernández Martínez, undeniably a fascist, was also a little odd. He is remembered, among many other things, for stringing colored lights throughout San Salvador, believing they would cure smallpox, then rampant in the capital. He held séances in his home and eagerly recommended drinking colored water to cure all illness. After he fell from power in 1944 he went to Honduras where, in 1966, he was stabbed to death by his driver, the son of one of the many thousands of Salvadorans Hernández Martínez had caused to be murdered.

The year 1932 brought a ham-handed communist uprising, whose violence was quickly surpassed by the government exacting a horrible revenge in massacres.*

By the 1960s the beginnings of what became the rebel armies of the 1980s were forming, adding to the national polarization. The resulting alphabet soup of acronyms of groups with various approaches and beliefs made more noise than difference until they met in Cuba and unified as the FMLN in 1980.†

Meanwhile, the paramilitary ORDEN, a creature of the military rule of Julio Rivera, was founded in 1961 with advice from the U.S. military. It became the Salvadoran military's eyes and ears, tasked with discovering and eliminating rural leftist activity, often with machetes. It was a precursor to the death squads of later years.

In 1965 all military and paramilitary information systems were unified, and they had some 100,000 agents at various levels working nationwide. This meant that 1 in 50 Salvadorans nationwide was a government snitch or enforcer, usually helping to repress members of their own social class. In the countryside, where ORDEN flourished, the ratio was substantially higher.‡

The Armed Forces of National Resistance, or FARN, and other leftist groups increased kidnappings of public figures, foreign diplomats, local and foreign businessmen and other

---

* Even today the Indian population in El Salvador remains tiny because of the killings. Martí became a rebel icon, and the guerrilla organization Farabundo Martí National Liberation Front, which won elected power in 2009, still bears his name.

† Statistics compiled for seven years after an abortive 1972 coup attempt showed a tenfold increase in political assassinations and a doubling of the number of disappeared suspected leftists.

‡ ORDEN, which means "order" in Spanish, was disbanded, at least officially, after the 1979 coup that threw out Gen. Carlos Humberto Romero.

high-dollar hostages, often demanding ransoms in the millions of dollars and publication of rebel tracts abroad.*

Gradually, leftist groups, who had much of their strength in student and labor organizations, began heading to the hills.

In 1980 the government closed the campus of the National University for four years. They claimed, with some plausibility, that it was a recruiting and training ground for rebels.

Some of us sneaked onto the campus soon after the closure and found some classroom blackboards still covered with diagrams for bomb-making.

Amid the growing crisis, cooler heads still tried to prevail.

Duarte had slipped back into the country in 1974 from exile in Venezuela to back an anti-military coalition in local elections, but the rigging was such that the coalition opted out.

They made a try for the presidency in 1977 but decided that conditions were too dangerous to run Duarte, who had returned to Venezuela.

The coalition picked instead a retired colonel, Ernesto Clairmont, to oppose Romero, but that vote was at least as crooked as the one five years earlier.

In 1977 the government passed the Law for the Defense and Guarantee of Public Order, removing most impediments to government violence against civilians.

---

* One famous hostage was South African Ambassador Archibald Dunn in late 1979. The price tag was $20 million for the 61-year-old diplomat, known to be in bad health. Pressed for evidence that Dunn was even alive, the rebels at one point released a photo of him holding that day's newspaper, then a common form of hostage verification. It was some 10 months after the Dunn kidnapping that the rebels said he was dead. Whether they killed him, as guerrillas reportedly did with some others whose ransom demands were not met, or he died of his infirmities was never clear.

When thousands of Salvadorans gathered at the downtown Plaza Libertad to protest the 1977 election results, a government attack left at least 50 casualties, including Clairmont.

Lore has it that as Clairmont was being loaded into a National Red Cross ambulance he was heard to say, in effect, "This is not the end. It is only the beginning."

"The beginning" only got worse.

As the war gathered momentum the then-rather-lonely voice of U.S. Ambassador Robert White tried to tell Washington and Salvadorans that until mushrooming human-rights abuses were dealt with, all the agrarian and other reforms in the world weren't going to cool off the conflict. He was recalled to Washington by the Reagan White House.

Other ambassadors had delivered similar messages to deaf ears.

I first wound up in El Salvador very briefly and almost by accident in late July of 1979 after the Sandinista win in Nicaragua. The airport in Nicaragua remained closed to commercial flights and leaving usually meant going to the airport and hanging out, hoping to mooch space on anything headed to where we could connect for home, which for me at the time was Mexico City.

I recall seeing American and Cuban planes parked almost side by side as ground crews offloaded hand trucks full of food and other supplies, a portent of future disagreement.

And there was a silver stretch DC-8 cargo jet with no markings that someone said belonged to the Salvadoran Red Cross—in retrospect, very doubtful.

After some palavering we got permission to board and sat on the floor with maybe 20 other people, hanging onto ropes amid a swirl of spilled red beans and corn as the jet made the short hop from Managua to San Salvador.

In mid-flight the loadmaster asked us if we wouldn't like to visit the cockpit for a few minutes to see how things were done. On our return to the cargo bay two passengers said that while we were in the cockpit a few of the other passengers had been quickly tucked away in some overhead space.*

I spent a couple of days in San Salvador, but the pressures remained pretty much out of sight. I left with little understanding of what was then in play, but there were clues.

The city still had meter maids, but they were packing submachine guns.

Ragged-looking women and kids along the street sold cigarettes and aspirin tablets one at a time. At night pick-up trucks bearing apparent civilians with automatic rifles prowled the narrow downtown streets, looking carefully at the pedestrians.

Television broadcasting seemed generally devoid of anything resembling political opposition. Attempts at friendly conversation usually ended or the topic was changed when politics came up. Who was this gringo? People weren't rude or visibly cowed, but something in the air, something felt, rather than seen, hinted that the best path was the straight and narrow one.

There was no visible "heavy hand," but the White Hand, Mano Blanco, was making is presence known as a death squad.

On the surface it all seemed orderly. Very orderly.

---

* Who they may have been, or why the "Salvadoran Red Cross" plane with its American pilots and crew was whisking them out of newly Sandinista Nicaragua to El Salvador, we never discovered.

The city had (and has) some of Central America's better restaurants, for the few who could afford them. There was still a nightlife of sorts, and theaters, museums, and art galleries, like anyplace else.

Record stores put their speakers on the sidewalk and cranked up the current hit, "Woman in Love" by Donna Summer or Barbra Streisand, and blared it nonstop, mixing discordantly in the street with ABBA's "Chiquitita." The two songs remain in my head.

It was only a few weeks after we met the couple at the check-out counter that we were back in El Salvador at the beginning of many long stays interrupted by coveted trips home, to neighboring countries with troubles of their own, or to Guatemala to graze in a pharmacy hoping to purge whatever it was we had.

When we returned for the long haul somehow El Salvador seemed different.

Within a short time we all knew how different.

How very different.

Page One

COVERING THE WAR in El Salvador was a seat up-close and on the aisle for the last bloody brawl of the Cold War. We covered a nation at war with itself, whose factions were proxies for two superpowers. It was something few would ever see up close, or would want to see again.

Foreign journalists covering the long, painful conflict found themselves in the unusual role of covering, often at the same time, both sides of it. Neither the guerrillas nor the government loved us very much, but in a war neither side could have supported for long on its own, both desperately needed to curry favor and aid from abroad. Had either side been forced to support the war on its own, without Soviet Bloc and U.S. involvement, the conflict might have ended much sooner. It lasted for 12 years.

We were an odd and varied bunch, some eventually resident there, some nearly so, some who dropped in now and then or only once, some fresh from the revolution next door in Nicaragua or, less recently, from Vietnam. A few had filtered in from the Middle East, some spoke no Spanish, some had never heard a bullet *ka-whing* past.[*]

Some stumbled off the plane misty-eyed with idealism, thinking the whole thing was a game. For Salvadorans it was a life or death matter for which dozens, sometimes scores might die in a single day. It was not a game.

---

[*] A bracing experience when you consider the alternative.

Joseph Frazier

The story of the Salvadoran war was page-one material for years, and journalistic competition was cut-throat. However, we often cooperated or worked together in small groups—if only for safety and the fact that, contrary to the opinion of New York editing desks, we couldn't be in eight places at once. Often getting to just one place was impossible. We kept an eye on and out for one another.

A few burned out and went home. Too many of us were killed there. In crossfire, which was mercifully rare, we felt like cockroaches on a dance floor. Nobody was going to stop while we tried to get out of the way.

Since those years, coverage of El Salvador has gone dark. El Salvador once drew America's top diplomatic talent and a raft of news coverage. It is a backwater today, much as it was before it began to explode. It was, and is now again, just another splotch on a map most Americans have never studied.

It was in about 1981, when El Salvador was in full roar, that I went briefly back to Mexico City, where I lived at the time. Our bureau chief, the late Eloy Aguilar, asked me to drive up to McAllen, Texas, to smuggle in some computer parts, a 1,500-mile round trip some of us made fairly often.

At a motel pool I was chatting with another guest, an accountant if memory serves, and he asked me what I did.

"El Salvador?" he responded. "I'm not really up to date on Scandinavia."

Most of us hit the ground running in El Salvador. Signs of the war were everywhere, of course, but some, including myself, probably should have identified the real issues more quickly.

We began knitting it together as the bodies showed up in ever-greater numbers and as we watched day-to-day life more carefully. The signs were everywhere.

In the capital, the poor, many displaced from the countryside, lived out of sight in crude huts of plywood and sometimes cardboard, hastily thrown together in the *barrancas*, or steep, terraced gullies, that zigzagged through the edges of the city.

On any given morning a boy in an immaculate pressed white shirt (how did he do that?) might surface over the barranca rim and head, maybe barefoot, down the street, a seemingly happy little guy with a ready wave and smile, chewing on an acidic green mango and heading who knew where.

Charming.

Most of us soon realized that the mango was breakfast and maybe lunch. Dinner, even. In the early years, we didn't think to follow him back home.

Rumors fly like shrapnel in wartime, but El Salvador soon became far more than a rumor mill as the dead turned up along roadsides, in peasant huts, dumped down wells, outside union halls, at the edges of crude cemeteries, and in fashionable parking lots.

Many conscripted Salvadoran soldiers, some of whom I knew to have been humane and sensitive, faced the same fate.

One night in roughly 1985 COPREFA, the Salvadoran army's press office, more than invited us to the rooftop of a forgotten building where they had laid out the bodies of about 30 Salvadoran soldiers killed in a recent battle.

This, we were told, was the handiwork of the guerrillas. This, we thought quietly, was what happens in wars.

A sergeant walked up and down the line of bodies, straddling them, whacking a machete across the bellies to free whooshes of built-up gas as they continued to bloat in the warm Salvadoran night.

Some laughed about it later, while others of us began to wonder if our basic human sensitivity wasn't being eroded, if this sort of thing shouldn't leave some huge, indelible mark.

Information from "official" sources of any kind was often dubious, and access to where things were happening for a firsthand look was sometimes blocked by troops of one persuasion or another.

We gnawed through mountains of spin and did the best we could. There remained for a short time a 1950s-style naïveté that told us if the U.S. government was telling us something, it must be true.

The facts on the ground quickly educated us otherwise.

The difference between us and working-class Salvadorans was that we could hop on a plane out. It was their home and they had to live with what went on around them.

After awhile the Salvadoran war became akin to a drug to many of us, and so we didn't leave. We woke up in the morning and we had to have it.

A dozen years earlier in another nasty brawl across the Pacific, orders for home and a flight date were cause for a king-hell party, time to throw the house out the window.

I can recall several colleagues I drove the 25 or so miles south out of San Salvador to the international airport at Comalapa as they left for other assignments. Some were in tears. I don't remember if I was when my turn came.

But I do remember faces, lots of them.

John Hoagland, 36, a *Newsweek* photographer and a California surfer guy with an infectious grin and bushy blond moustache, was on patrol near the town of Suchitoto with government troops in March of 1984 when they hit a guerrilla ambush.

They dove for cover behind a tree. "We got sprayed with bullets and one of them got him," said Bob Nickelsburg of *Time* magazine, who was with Hoagland. He quoted John as saying only, "I've been hit." His last words. It was an hour before shooting died down and Nickelsburg could move his wounded companion.

Word spread quickly in San Salvador that John had been badly wounded, and most of us headed to Hospital Policlínico to await his arrival. People who had been there long enough to know better talked of miracles. Hoagland didn't make it. Doctors removed a single 7.62mm bullet, which could have come from either side, from Hoagland's body.

The Rev. Peter O'Neil, an Irish Franciscan priest who lived in rebel turf 100 or so miles northeast of the capital and was a close friend of John's, said at the brief ceremony in the capital that "it was John's work to seek the truth and communicate it. When we think of our dead friend we may ask ourselves if it is worth giving our life for the truth. But if some are not willing, the truth cannot be communicated."

Hoagland had an earthier take on things. At least once when he was accused of being shy of the truth he hefted the camera from around his neck and said, with his trademark goofy grin, "Esta madre no dice mentiras."—"This mother doesn't lie."

There were other fatalities too in the first five years or so of the war:

A New York–based French photographer, **Olivier Rebbot**, was hit by guerrilla gunfire as he accompanied government troops in the northeastern department, or province, of Morazán. He died several days later in a hospital.

Joseph Frazier

Ian Mates, a South African television cameraman working for UPITN, was hit in the head by shrapnel from a mine north of the capital and died the next day.

Ignacio Rodríguez Terrazas, a reporter for the leftist Mexico City newspaper *Uno más uno,* was hit after he got out of his car during a firefight near the capital ahead of the 1982 constituent assembly elections and died the next day.

A Chilean cameraman was killed filming violence surrounding the same election.

More, including at least four other Americans, died in Nicaragua and Honduras.

ABC correspondent **Bill Stewart** was killed when he was shot point-blank by a Nicaraguan soldier as he lay facedown and unarmed in Managua in 1979.

In 1983 *Los Angeles Times* correspondent **Dial Torgerson** and photographer **Richard Cross** died instantly when their car hit a mine on a lonely road along the Honduran border with Nicaragua, a focal point of the U.S.-backed Contra War aimed at toppling the Sandinistas.

But it wasn't all random.

During the election campaign of 1982 a four-man Dutch TV crew headed—secretly, they thought—to a rendezvous with the rebel Popular Liberation Forces in the rough-and-tumble northern department of Chalatenango.

All were shot to death in an army ambush on a parched, remote hillside shortly after being dropped off by a driver.

Soon after, provisional President Duarte appeared in a surprise visit to the Camino Real Hotel, where most of us were staying, to say he had ordered the military to protect journalists but could not guarantee their safety. He said the soldiers did not know the Dutch crew was in the area, a

Photographer Olivier Rebbot mortally wounded, tended by fellow photographer Harry Mattison. Photo: Murry Sill.

claim the United Nations Truth Commission roundly refuted years later.

"If you go where we cannot protect you, how can we protect you?" he asked. "If you walk with a guerrilla patrol, you run all the dangers."

The government autopsies of the four, plus a fifth victim, were concluded in less than an hour total and were icily clinical.

Cameraman **Jacobs Van Willensen**, multiple gunshot wounds that left his skull and brain destroyed.

Soundman **Hans Lodewijk Ter Laag**, shot twice in the side with bullets that struck his heart and left lung.

Director **Jan Kornelius Kuyper**, shot twice in the face with stomach wounds that could have come from grenade shrapnel.

Mexico-based newsman **Jacobus Andres Koster**, "Koos" to all of us, shot through the left leg and eye.

AP photographer Pat Hamilton and I were looking for them along a steep, rough road in the area when Pat spotted piles of bloody clothing, some with Dutch labels, and drag marks indicating something heavy had been moved to the side of the road.

We and two others found the bodies that evening, wrapped in clear plastic, in a makeshift cinder-block morgue at a municipal cemetery near downtown San Salvador.

The post-war Truth Commission concluded that there was ample evidence that the four, known to have done stories favorable to the rebels in the past, walked into an ambush set for them by the military and that military officials obstructed later investigations and otherwise refused to cooperate.

And there was **John Sullivan**, a 26-year-old journalist from New Jersey on assignment, he said, for *Hustler* magazine, which even then sounded improbable.

He vanished from his room at the Sheraton Hotel in San Salvador shortly after he got there in December of 1980. It was rumored that he had said a little too much a little too loudly on the flight down from Miami about his hope to make contact with the guerrillas.

In 1983 bones found along a roadside were identified by lab tests as his. His killers were never identified.

There were others.

Men we assumed to be rightist militia sometimes would drop by the lobby bar at the Camino Real, where we often gathered at night to unwind and swap lies. On one occasion one of these men struck up a conversation with two of us and pulled his jacket back to reveal a large pistol in his belt. He said, in essence, that we seemed like a couple of really nice guys and it would be a shame if something were to happen to us.

Several of us got pre-dawn phone calls and heard only the *click, click, click* of the hammer of an empty revolver. Then silence.

It was around this time that an alleged "death list" was being circulated by a rightist paramilitary group that may have existed in name only.

We took it with a little salt since all or nearly all of the 35 names on it were misspelled. A few co-workers were miffed because they were left off, and custom T-shirts began showing up: "Death List: If you ain't on it, you ain't shit!"

Through it all we bobbed and weaved around congressional delegations, or "codels," that flew down from D.C. to get to the bottom of all this, by George.

There were exceptions, but most seemed to go by the U.S. Embassy for the obligatory briefings, meet with a Salvadoran official or two, take a safe and scripted tour, then head home, often on a government jet.

Before they left after their quickie visits a few would call a news conference to tell us what was going on in El Salvador. We, of course, hung on every word.

They could have bought a newspaper back home or phoned down and gotten pretty much the same information, but it was nice of them to show up. Unlike in D.C., the winter weather in El Salvador could be beautiful. Or they could have talked to us. We knew plenty.

Today people would dub such "fact-finding missions" as boondoggles and they would be right.

The hometown papers often wanted us to drop everything, transmit photos and write all about the visits of their worthies. As a wire service we did that to a reasonable degree, but most of the visits could politely be called a pain.

Other problems came from unpredictable sources rooted in the fact that our little corner of Latin America remained pretty much unknown to most Americans despite years of headlines, photos, and network newscasts.

This was combined with the assumption that those of us on the scene, marinated in the story for years, knew far less than our superiors in New York and Washington.

Most had a favorite "groaner" tale, and we sometimes would gather around a jug and trade them back and forth.

Here are two I remember all too well.

The 1982 constituent assembly election to pick the people who would write yet another Salvadoran constitution was in bloody chaos as guerrillas tried to block the voting, if only to prove they were strong enough to do so (they weren't). There

```
...TOS CON LOS RESPONSABLES DEL DESPRESTIGIO INTERNACIONAL CAUSADO A NUEST
ARMADA Y PRINCIPALES COMPLICES DEL COMUNISMO SOVIETICO CUBANO SANDINISTA Q
RE APODERAR DE NUESTRA AMADA PATRIA:
   1  KAREN DE YOUNG, REPORTER DEL WASHINTON POUST DE LOS EEUU.
   2  RAIMON BONER DEL NEW YORK TIMES DE LOS EEUU.
   3  CHIRLEY CRISTIAN DEL MIAMI HERALD DE LOS EEUU.
   4  ALAN RAIDIN DEL NEW YORK TIMES DE LOS EEUU.
   5  HOWARD LANE DE LA EMBAJADA DE LOS EEUU EN NUESTRA PATRIA
   6  DON CRNUSH DE LA TELEVISIVA NBC
   7  EDUARDO VASQUEZ BEQUER DE GUATEMALA DE LA AP
   8  GARY PETERSEN DE LOS ESTADOS UNIDOS DE LA AP
   9  VICENTE MORALES DE MEXICO DE LA AP.
   10 JOE FRAZER DE LOS ESTADOS UNIDOS DE LA AP
   11 JON NEUJAGEN DE LOS ESTADOS UNIDOS DE LA UPI
   12 RAUL BELTRAN TRAIDOR SALVADOREÑO DE LA UPI
   13 JUAN O TAMAYO MEXICANO DE LA UPI
   14 CRIST DIKINSON DE LOS ESTADOS UNIDOS DE WASHINTON POUST.
   15 CARLOS ROSAS GAITAN GUATEMALTECO DE LA NBC DE LOS ESTADOS UNIDOS.
   16 ERIC NEPOMUCENO DE MEXICO BRASIL
   17 XU YAOMING CHINO QUE VIVE EN MEXICO
   18 VICTOR BARBOSA PONCD MEXICANO DE IPS
   20 RAUL MONZON TRAIDOR SALVADOREÑO (renuncio)
   21 ENRIQUE CASTRO TRAIDOR SALVADOREÑO
   22 FRANCISCO GUZMAN TRAIDOR SALVADOREÑO
   23 RENE ARMANDO CONTRERAS TRAIDOR SALVADOREÑO
   24 JOSE NAPOLEON GONSALEZ TRAIDOR SALVADOREÑO
   25 VICTOR HUGO MATA TRAIDOR SALVADOREÑO
   26 DANILO VELADO TRAIDOR SALVADOREÑO.
   27 MARIO HERNANDEZ HONDUREÑO DE LA PRENSA
   28 ROBIN LOID DE LOS ESTADOS UNIDOS DE LA NBC.
   29 JHON KELLY DE LOS ESTADOS UNIDOS DE LA VOZ DE AMERICA
   30 ALMA PRIETO DE MEXICO DE EL GUARDIAN DE INGLATERRA
   31 JHON JOGLAND DE LOS ESTADOS UNIDOS DE LA UPI
   32 HARRI MATISON DE LOS ESTADOS UNIDOS DE NEWSWEK
   33 SILVIO VOCANERA DE BRASIL DE JOURNAL DE BRASIL
   34 CRISTOPHER WINER INGLES DE LA BBC
   35 DOMINGO REX MEXICANO DE LA TELEVISIVA ABC
ESTA ES LA PRIMERA PARTE DE SEUDO PERIODISTAS AL SERVICIO DE LA SUBVERSION
NAL QUE HAN SIDO CONDENADOS A MUERTE POR LOS PATRIOTAS DE NUESTRA ORGANIZAC
ESTAMOS INVESTIGANDO A LOS OTROS QUE VAN Y VIENEN A NUESTRA PATRIA PARA S
SERVICIO DE QUIEN ESTAN. M U E R T E  A  L O S  T R A I D O R E S A  L A
C I A.
       ALIANZA ANTICOMUNISTA DE EL SALVADOR SIMPATIZANTE DE LA GLORIOSA BRIG
       MAXIMILIANO HERNANDEZ MARTINEZ
SAN SALVADOR 10 DE MARZO DE 1982.
```

This copy of the death list surfaced during a 2009 reunion of colleagues from El Salvador. Most names are comically misspelled. At least I made it into the top ten. It reads, in part (some words are obscured by years of copying): "These are those responsible for the international loss of prestige of our army and the main accomplices of Soviet, Cuban and Sandinista communism trying to take over the country. They are the first among pseudo-journalists in the service of subversion…who have been sentenced to death by the patriots of our organization. We are investigating others who come and go in our country. Death to traitors. (Signed) The Anticommunist Alliance of El Salvador in Support of the Glorious Maximiliano Hernández Martínez Brigade."

were several hundred journalists, TV crews, technicians, etc. in-country for what had sadly become a feeding frenzy.

In the middle of it all we got a scorching call from the New York photo desk demanding to know why we hadn't filed election-day photos of the presidential candidates. By God, we were going to roast slowly if we didn't send them out ASAP.

It took half an hour to calm him down and make him understand this wasn't even a presidential election, and that if he had bothered to read any of the tons of stories we had been writing for the past six weeks he would know it.

Equally amusing, in retrospect only, was a miserably stormy night in Managua, Nicaragua, when we sent something brief about unconfirmed reports of a major dust-up between the Sandinista army and the American-backed contra forces near the isolated town of Wiwilí, which was often in the thick of the fighting.

Of course the phone rang. Why weren't we up there getting photos of all this? I don't know if it was the same guy we had dealt with in El Salvador—I'd hate to think there were two of them—but the problem was the same.

He was told, very patiently, that it was at least a four-hour drive over horrible roads that might not be passable even in daylight and that might well be mined, and that once we were there there would be no way to transmit photos over phone connections that could charitably be described as primitive. There was a high probability of an ambush.

"I don't see your problem," came the reply. "I got a Nicaragua map in my hands. Looks like about Baltimore to Washington to me."

The touchiness of the day-to-day situation in the region was not without its benefits, however. Very few "suits" came down to tell us how to do our jobs.

Most editors knew their job and ours and didn't ask us to take unnecessary chances. The late Nate Polowetzky, who was foreign editor at the time and was himself a veteran of turbulent times in many countries, was constantly telling us, "It isn't worth it. There'll be other stories."

Most of us quickly developed a knack for staying out of jams. It worked, mostly, and relied heavily on gut feelings.

If something doesn't look right, get out or stay out. And never assume you know more than the local people, because you don't.

Most of us made it a point to stop in markets of small towns, make a couple of small purchases, get to know a few people who, at times, warned us off certain roads we mentioned we were planning to travel. Mines, they said.

They usually knew, and if they liked you they probably would tell you. It wasn't hard to "read" a village after a while. If one seemed virtually empty on a normally busy market day, or if there was an unexplained military presence by one side or the other, there usually was a reason. Stick your toe in first.

At times we cursed the fate that would catch us overnight or for days in some of the poorer, more isolated villages until we realized, for the umpteenth time, the residents lived under these miserable conditions every day.

Back in the capital, we had formed the SPCA, or Salvador Press Corps Association, complete with credentials and T-shirts, both highly prized today. The government had its own press credentials, but the SPCA card usually was enough to get past rebel checkpoints or roadblocks.

We placed the letters "TV" in masking tape on the sides, windows, and roofs of our cars, and that probably prevented

many of us from getting shot up. Later we found that some unmarked military vehicles were using the same markings. I recall the SPCA, which had no real standing anywhere, raising minor hell over the military's use of the "TV" markings and we did not hear of repeat instances.

We developed strong ties with our Salvadoran staff members, who could navigate the local peculiarities far better than we could, and who seemed to know nearly everybody we might want to talk to. It was, again, a very small country.

Some of them remain among my closest friends to this day.

At day's end, there was often a *cucharada* (a shot of liquor in El Salvador's rich vernacular) which rarely ended with just one and sometimes moved from office to office.

Nicaragua's excellent Flor de Caña rum was the anodyne of choice when we could find it, and we usually could, sometimes too easily and often. And there were plenty of times when such a respite, or one like it, seemed essential to cut the dust and the tension.

Practical jokes also helped.

Page One

In 1982 during a memorable lunchtime at the Camino, whose menu we came to know by heart during the curfew times, tension was fiddle-string tight because of competition.

There may have been 75 or 80 journalists, TV cameramen, and photographers in the cafeteria and lobby keeping an eye on each other and planning how to process the tidbits they had in hand.

So three of us ran like the wind through the lobby out to a car and roared out of the parking lot. The hotel emptied, and we were followed by a cortege of TV vans and other cars full of our friends and competitors, all sure that we had stumbled across the second coming of Christ, or maybe something better, and would have photos.

The crazy caravan snaked down a main street and up into the Escalon district, where we pulled over and walked inside a simple but good Mexican restaurant for lunch. Our followers hit the brakes and nearly rear-ended each other then realized they had been had. Somehow only we thought it was very funny.

When my main print competition headed out to the airport to pick up a piece of visiting brass from New York or Washington, several conspirators gathered up all the empty booze bottles we could find and left them in a pile outside his office door to greet them on their return.

He didn't speak to us for a couple of days. It was those little things...

A photographer who might not appreciate being named here came down from a long and dusty stint in the mountains in the mid 1980s with several rolls of film (in those pre-digital times) and vanished with them and a fifth of Flor de Caña into the hotel bathroom, which had been light-sealed and tricked out as a darkroom.

He emerged an hour or so later with the bottle nearly empty and a stack of some of the most drop-dead beautiful prints we had seen in some time.

How, we asked, could this be?

He gave a trademark twirl to his moustache and said, "Frazier—*anybody* can do it sober!"

Yes, okay, many of us got drunk a lot, but I don't know of anybody who wrote for publication in that condition. Do a roughcut, set it aside, and go over it in the morning.

It was not considered prudent to kid around with Salvadoran troops, and even less so with members of the security forces.

But photographers back then had to travel with huge metal cases containing enlargers, developing equipment, chemicals, and more.

On entering the country a national guardsman ordered a case to be opened and saw a quantity of white powder spilled in the bottom. It was, in fact, fixer, a chemical used in black-and-white photography.

Certain he had found a huge cocaine stash, he wet his finger, dipped it into the powder, and put a generous sample in his mouth.

I was not present for this performance, but those who were said the "aha!" moment was theirs, not his.

It worked both ways.

An arriving co-worker recalls an airport security agent asking him if he was, in fact, a *periodista,* a journalist.

He allowed he was.

The soldier took a marking pen from his pocket and drew a black "X" over the guy's heart and walked away.

Labor Ministry, San Salvador: A leftist demonstrator peers from the former labor ministry, which either the Popular Revolutionary Bloc or FARN (Armed Forces of National Resistance), both major players in the larval stages of the rebel movement, occupied in 1979. Our visit to the rebels occupying the ministry nearly got myself and photographer Pat Hamilton, who took the above photo, killed. We had talked our way inside the ministry that night, and when we came out the National Police grabbed us and walked us down an alley with guns in our backs. I had a small tape recorder with a cassette in it that on one side had recordings from a demonstration earlier that day. On the other side was a news conference on oil prices held days earlier in Mexico City. The cop grabbed the recorder and hit the play button. We then listened to some toad blow his nose at length about oil prices. That was a wonderful feeling. I used a clean, new tape each day after that. Photo: Pat Hamilton.

Transmission of stories was by glacially slow phone lines or Telex—ours went to Mexico first—until the first laptops began appearing. This led to other problems.

There was no prior censorship then, but I suspected as did others, that whatever we sent on phone lines or Telex was zipped through the government press office before it got to its destination.

Doubt vanished after I wrote a piece about a guerrilla leader who had changed sides and agreed to cooperate with the military.

I recall writing that he appeared sleep-deprived and almost catatonic as he told his story, and that he may have been put through God knows what before we got to him.

I was called by the military press headquarters and roundly chewed out for writing such blasphemy.

The only thing was, the story had not been published yet anywhere.

Welcome to El Salvador in the 1980s.

Paz Wore a Bullet

AT ABOUT DAWN, when the government's recurring shoot-to-kill curfew lifted, rattletrap station wagons tricked out as hearses belched, coughed blue smoke, and lurched from hole-in-the-wall funeral parlors in San Salvador's ragged sectors onto side streets and back roads on their macabre morning patrols.

Theirs was a run for the money, to where rightist death squads usually dumped victims after a night's work. The back door popped open, two men loaded up the remains, slammed the door, and continued on their run. It was 1981 and the squads were in full roar as the country's civil war picked up momentum and the established right reacted.

By midmorning the drivers, hoping for the burial business, were back at their parlors waiting for people making rounds of their own, seeking missing friends or relatives. If unidentified bodies were found first by government patrols, they usually were buried on the spot as unknowns.[*]

A man who called himself Armando Paz tried to get there first.

The diminutive Paz, who looked 30 or so, drove a daily 60-mile route around and through the capital to find and photograph death-squad victims for church and human-rights groups that kept the pictures on file for people seeking missing friends or relatives.

---

[*] Thirty years later faded and sagging roadside crosses and simple floral offerings maintained by family members still marked a few of those.

Paz wore a bullet, rifling grooves intact, on a chain around his neck, the bullet rumored to have killed his father. Paz would never tell me.

"Sometimes people will find bodies and put up crosses made of sticks," he said on his rounds one day in early 1981. "We look for those. And we look for packs of dogs and circling vultures."

It was easy to figure out who the killers were, he said. "The left kills its victims quickly. The right tortures theirs first."

Handheld acetylene blowtorches were favored, although they were more common still next door in Guatemala, where torturers signed their victims' chests. Were they alive at the time? Maybe.

Paz said pictures taken by his predecessor showed most victims face down in the dirt, useless for identification.

"You needed someone who could get close to the face. Nobody else would do it. I turn all the heads so they face the camera. It's a job you do," he shrugged. He said his daily search usually produced at least six victims. His one-day record as of then was 47.

Some victims were taken by their killers to el Puerto del Diablo, the Devil's Door, a park-like place on a cliff south of the capital. It is a pleasant enough park today, if you can ignore its past.

Death-squad members would throw bodies off the cliff. They would land a few hundred feet down, becoming the problem of Panchimalco, a quiet indigenous village at the cliff's base. Some didn't make it all the way. Paz boasted of a keen nose, and volunteers would go down on ropes to investigate.

A too-frequent sight in San Salvador, 1979.
Photo: Pat Hamilton.

Paz once found eight bodies at the base of the cliff. Three were buried as unknowns in a common grave in a cluster of weeds and already-fading painted wooden crosses in the town cemetery.

María Ercillia had identified one of the three from Paz's photos as her missing husband and had come to claim his remains. She had paid $280 for a coffin, a fortune in rural El Salvador.

Paz and a determinedly anonymous human-rights worker who said she was Dutch talked quietly with Sra. Ercillia. Freelance grave diggers, who had each bargained on the spot for the equivalent of about $12 and a bottle of Muñeco, a cheap, corrosive sugar liquor redolent of diesel, went to work after fortifying themselves with hefty gulps.

They would need it.

"What was he wearing?" asked one, chest deep in the grave.

"Black pants with stripes."

"Dental work?"

"He had small, straight teeth, pretty teeth," she answered quietly. A digger held up a piece of jawbone and fabric from the reeking pit. She approached slowly.

"Leave him where he is," she said.

The workers rinsed their hands with some of the remaining rotgut before filling in the grave. The widow said she could return the casket. Passers-by grumbled that the government at least should provide the large plastic bags used as coffins in such cases.

So things went in El Salvador in a grinding war trumpeted from abroad as part of a global East-West struggle but which, for many Salvadorans, meant little more than new ways to die.

In El Salvador in the 1980s it wasn't hard to wake up dead, or disappeared, as the saying went. People who knew the wrong people or had the wrong enemies or were heard saying the wrong thing or were reported by a rival in love or business to have said the wrong thing or had the wrong job or stumped for a union could be dragged from bed in the small hours by death squads and shot. Often the family was awakened and forced to watch. Nobody was immune, not even priests. More than a dozen clerics were killed in a mistaken belief that the church was a leftist monolith.

An otherwise reasonable New York editor with years of foreign-service experience kept asking, "What does the average Salvadoran think of all this? Give me a 'man on the street' story." We finally convinced him that if the average Salvadoran had two working brain cells, he kept his mouth shut.

There were occasional no-questions-asked shoot-to-kill curfews, often at 7 p.m., to try to deny the rebels the night. Death squads somehow worked freely through the night in spite of the curfew.

One Sunday morning journalists heading down a main street for the cathedral a mile or so away to cover the archbishop's often-feisty homily, the kind that got him murdered, counted 17 bodies. There was no rubbernecking. Traffic moved normally past the head wounds to the extent that it ever moved normally. On bad mornings kids walking to school or women headed to market stepped over or walked around bodies to get there. Overheard discussions often involved only arguments over what kind of weapon had been used.

As Salvadorans hardened to the new reality, a sort of black humor arose. For example:

Two national guardsmen watched an old man totter up the street toward his home. One checked his watch, raised his

G-3 assault rifle, and dropped the old fellow in his tracks. "Curfew," he explained.

"But it's only 6:45," protested his comrade.

"I know where he lives," the first said. "He never would have made it."

Thunderous coughs in the night rolled across the capital as guerrillas blew up power poles and detonated car bombs.

It worked this way: A stolen car was packed with explosives and fixed with a time fuse. A driver hustled it across the capital to an intended target, parked, and ran.

One rainy night a flash lit up the sky near the Camino Real Hotel, where much of the press corps stayed and had offices, partly for collective security, partly because there was usually electricity.

A large patch was laid bare by the bomb, but the main kerfuffle was a block or so away, where firemen, neighbors, the Salvadoran Red Cross and National Police gathered.

The bomb had gone off early, blowing the driver through the top of the car, through the air, and down through the red tile roof of a house.[*]

As Red Cross workers literally scooped him into plastic bags, the family in the next room continued eating dinner as if nothing had happened. El Salvador could be like that.

The American Embassy, which had more control than was immediately evident, frequently warned the security forces, the military, and much of the oligarchy that sponsored the death squads that human-rights abuses had reached a point that could jeopardize essential American military aid, and that

---

[*] A later botched effort slammed the driver's body against the side of a house, leaving its outline for a time on the white stucco.

it was repressive attitudes toward the poor that helped trigger the war.

Ambassadors had been delivering similar sporadic cautions off and on since the 1960s. The most vocal was Ambassador White, replaced early in the Reagan administration because he favored a diplomatic or negotiated solution over a military one.

Late in the Carter administration, after three American nuns and a lay Catholic social worker were murdered by Salvadoran National Guard troops in 1980, aid was cut briefly until Washington decided, not without reason, that the Cubans and Soviets were running arms to Salvadoran rebels with the happy cooperation of Nicaragua and resumed the flow of military help.

A major guerrilla offensive also got the new Reagan administration's attention. It was the first of many rebel "final offensives," which they would declare on a semi-regular basis.

The five National Guard soldiers convicted of killing the churchwomen were sentenced to 30 years in prison. Three had been released by 2011 for good behavior. The other two were due for release in 2015. The five were specifically excluded from protection under the 1993 general amnesty. Their superiors were never called to account.

However, in 2012 the United States was trying to deport two former ranking Salvadoran defense officials living legally in the United States to El Salvador.

Gen. José Guillermo García was defense minister in 1980 when the soldiers raped and murdered the churchwomen. Gen. Carlos Eugenio Vides Casanova was then head of the National Guard.

Both won civil suits and appeals brought by family members of the victims but lost lawsuits charging them with torture.

Meanwhile, those with the money, land, and power kept a grip on it in their usual and sometimes lethal ways.

In El Salvador, a nascent land reform effort and nationalization of banks and of key exports followed the Nicaraguan revolution. Another result of the revolution in Nicaragua was the unexpected coup in El Salvador led by two reform-minded Salvadoran military officers—who apparently didn't want to see their country go the way of Nicaragua, or who may have dreamt of more for themselves.

It may well have been an independent move but it brings to my mind the old wheeze, "Why aren't there military coups in Washington, D.C.? Because there is no American Embassy there." It is probable, in my mind at least, that they would not have tried the coup without at least a wink from an American Embassy that saw pressure building up fast.

However, the new measures of the provisional government after the coup riled the upper classes, who felt their way of life threatened. Then began the bloodiest years of the war.

Nationalizing key exports such as coffee meant producers sold to the government, which paid them in local currency, instead of selling their crops overseas and sending the dollars back out of the country for safekeeping. It wasn't the "Salvadoran way."

Contentious land reforms were intended to turn over parts of the largest land holdings to the peasants, paid for by government bonds.

Land inequality in the largely agricultural country was staggering. Before the coup, by some reckonings, 2 percent of the population owned 60 percent of the farmable land. They were hell-bent on keeping it.

Private militias and the Salvadoran National Guard, formed at the turn of the 20th century to help them keep things in check, enforced things.

Reform-minded peasants and agrarian reform workers were common targets. How many of the "disappeared" still lie in unmarked graves in fields and along roadsides and how many just fled the country may never be known.

In 1981 two American labor advisors, Michael Hammer and David Mark Pearlman, along with Salvadoran labor specialist José Rodolfo Viera, were mowed down by two members of the Salvadoran National Guard. These murders followed the killings of the three American churchwomen, and that of the Archbishop of San Salvador, Msgr. Óscar Arnulfo Romero.

Through all of this the American Embassy sent a monthly report to Washington, D.C., known in-house as the "grim-gram," which summarized political killings, mostly of civilians.

Embassy officials said privately that the number sometimes was in the 1,000 range at the height of the violence, but numbers generally were all over the chart from religious groups, human-rights organizations, and others. Some months, 1,000 seemed very low.

Regardless, the figures were numbingly high, each number representing a human being in a country where lots of people knew each other.

In October of 1980 María Magdalena Henríquez, spokeswoman for El Salvador's Nongovernmental Human Rights Commission, was kidnapped from her home by uniformed policemen hours after I had spent the morning interviewing her. Her body was found in a makeshift grave a couple of days later.

Commission administrator Ramón Valladares was killed three weeks later, shortly after meeting with a handful of foreign journalists.

Coincidence? More than 30 years later I can only hope so.

The State Department meanwhile was wooing a sometimes-skeptical Congress for more aid, and while much of this was going on, Congress was being assured through a "certification" process every six months that the rights problems were improving. It didn't look that way to most of us.

The deaths continued and Salvadorans tried to cope. Firefights could erupt from anywhere, from nowhere, downtown, on a rural road. Pharmacies sold high-octane Valium over the counter, one pill at a time. The military opened a brand-new mortuary.

Guerrillas blew a McDonalds, to them a toothsome symbol of Yanqui imperialism, out of the ground. Another McDonalds placed guards with automatic weapons outside to protect the place while the kiddies of the well-to-do—a long day's wage in the countryside wouldn't buy a Big Mac—romped in the play area or swatted at birthday piñatas.

A freelance photographer new to the ways of El Salvador began taking pictures, ignoring a guard's order to stop. So the guard shot him in the leg.

It was a time and place where if someone with a gun told you to do something, you probably ought to do it.

Wartime El Salvador was flush with weapons. Nobody knew where many of them came from. Some were relics from the 1969 border war with Honduras, others were purchased on the free-wheeling international arms market by rebels flush with ransom cash from pre-war kidnappings, and others were captured from government troops.

If you had a few dollars and wanted a firearm you could have it, have it and welcome.

Kids near San Francisco Gotera in the troubled eastern province of Morazán would offer hand grenades for a dollar or two. "New, never used," said one, trying not to laugh.

But many Salvadorans didn't seem to identify with the war, they just tried to survive it. It was "el problema," "la época," "the times in which we live, you see."

Artisans continued to produce and sell their wares. Art galleries still handled some very good local talent. You could head out in the morning to a combat zone, find classical music on the car radio, and be back in the capital in time to meet deadline and snag dinner.

But roadblocks or checkpoints could be around any bend, and it was often anybody's guess as to whose they were until the last minute.

Rebel forces sometimes declared and enforced a travel ban on rural highways or blew up bridges. Other times traffic was stopped, with drivers rolling into ditches as the two factions fought it out from opposite sides of the highway.

Guerrillas might ask for some sort of document or solicit a small "cooperation for the liberators." It was considered at least prudent to pony up a couple of colons. Cigarettes worked.

The war evolved into a stew of futility, people coping, dying, just trying to ride out a storm that offered few clear skies ahead.

It fed on itself. "When a man is murdered his brothers do two things," an American military advisor told me in about 1982. "They go to his funeral, and then they head to the hills to join the rebels."

Joseph Frazier

On a busy evening in about 1979 someone hurled a Molotov cocktail onto the steps of a columned Greek-style building in the downtown capital housing several lesser Cabinet offices.

Guards opened fire on crowds at a bus stop across the street, killing or injuring about 20 people. Like Inspector Clouseau, the war could be everywhere and nowhere.

Trucks carrying coffee beans, a main source of the country's serious money and peasant exploitation, to processing stations, were especially sweet targets. If the beans weren't processed soon after harvest, they began to ferment and became worthless. Tires were shot out, engine blocks were larded with bullets. For the rebels it was a two-fer. They dealt both the overall economy and The Man a stiff lick.

Parts of the country went for years with no electricity as rebels targeted power poles and high-voltage transmission lines and planted land mines to hamper repairs. American helicopters flew in replacement parts when they could. Again and again.

A man in the coffee-growing town of California, east of the capital, lamented that he had bought a refrigerator just before a blackout that lasted more than a year and never had a chance to use it.

People got by. Gasoline generators powered the lights in some homes and hospital operating rooms. Service-station operators rigged hand pumps to bring the gas from underground tanks for motorists when there was gas to sell.

Gasoline-truck drivers thought twice about making the run to war zones if they thought about it at all. That big red Texaco star on a tanker truck lumbering slowly toward the east made a tempting target for a rocket grenade.

To this day I don't know how the guerrillas hoped to win the hearts, minds, etc., of the remaining residents of the battered, bloodied eastern provinces by making their lives harder than they already were.

The rich got around wartime shortages. The poor knew them all too well. With the economy choking, President Duarte cut way back on permitted luxury imports such as wines, new vehicles, jewelry, and foreign foods to save scarce hard currency for essential imports such as medicines, oil, and fertilizer.

But the poor guy couldn't seem to win: his actions only triggered more protests from the well-dressed matrons of Escalón, San Benito, and other posh neighborhoods.

The sound of empty pans banging together, a traditional Latin American symbol of protest associated with the poor, would rise over a sea of signs denouncing Duarte for threatening national security, being a communist, being a bad Salvadoran, threatening "our way of life," and God knows what else.

But the matrons weren't carrying the signs or banging the pans. They brought their maids along to do that.

Coffee was (and remains) a Salvadoran mainstay, and the government, which now controlled its export, sent the best beans overseas for top dollar. What was left was still pretty good but not the *mero-mero,* the best.

Well-off Salvadorans who missed their mero-mero morning cup had it shipped back to them from friends abroad, usually Miami.

As they sipped it, children died.

Dollars, which in theory the Central Bank controlled, were made twice as expensive in local currency to discourage "capital flight"—sending them out of the country or spending them on nonessential imports (such as their own coffee?).

That meant higher prices in local currency for many imports, including medicines, setting most Salvadorans down yet another peg.

Exchange rates fluctuated, but rural wages often equaled about $1.60 a day for men and women, $1.40 for children and the handicapped. Industrial workers might get $3 a day in the cities, $2.80 in the countryside.

Gasoline, though, cost about what it did in the United States, and many imports cost more.

Even at those wages, groups of field hands would gather on a bridge or riverbank of an evening in the often-lawless east and wonder if they would be paid for their week's work. Sometimes the "agent" told them that the owner, often anonymous, had not sent the money. There were murmured suspicions that someone had trousered it, but things being the way they were, it was better to keep quiet. Maybe next week.*

Bullets weren't the only killers. Disease took a terrible toll, especially among the very young.

The Central Bank, of necessity, determined who could buy dollars for essential imports.

Many importers bypassed the bank and paid even higher black-market prices for dollars sent home by Salvadorans working abroad. In some towns such funds were the only source of new money.

---

* In the same east the guerrillas opened a campaign to kidnap or kill town officials from rightist parties in the run-up to the 1985 legislative elections. At least ten, probably more, in villages with conservative governments died. In San Jorge, two city officials were shot dead in city hall. Nearby, a boy about 12 years old recalled guerrillas taking his father, a minor municipal functionary, out of their home and how the boy pleaded for his release. The family asked at the time that I not use their names so I wrote nothing down. The kid recalled the rebels telling him not to worry, everything would be okay. Minutes later he heard the two shots.

Outside the main post office in the capital, people buying or selling dollars stood silently waving calculators and wads of local currency. You could negotiate.

Such back-alley deals, which became a cottage industry, sucked up dollars and put many imports, including life-saving medicines, beyond common reach.

Clusters of funeral parlors around often-basic local hospitals, which did the best they could, both bore witness and told a tale in themselves.

Stacks of tiny styrofoam coffins testified to a stunning childhood mortality rate, officially 41 per 1,000 live births, nowhere near the world's worst, but bad. Most doctors put it substantially higher, saying many such deaths were in rural areas and went unrecorded. (The United States rate is about 12 per 1,000 live births, still higher than in many developed countries.)

Bad water caused dysentery and cholera, both preventable, both major and rapid childhood killers. My memory of a small procession of young girls in white dresses carrying crosses and a tiny coffin through the streets of Usulután in the mid-1980s remains clear. Not one of the girls appeared to be more than ten years old.

Through it all El Salvador kept its slogan, "The Country with a Heart," and for all the bitterness and mayhem of the times, it could prove itself true, albeit in strange and isolated ways.

The concept of prisoners of war was often lost to both sides, especially to some government units. After an especially nasty fight on the southern edge of the department of Morazán, an officer spoke briefly to journalists and boasted of the rebels they had killed.

When we asked him about prisoners he looked at us as if we were from another country.* "Prisoners?"

But after a day of skirmishing amid Usulután cotton fields and mangrove swamps in 1982, guerrillas waved down a car with two journalists and asked us to take some army soldiers they had wounded to a government aid station or to their barracks for treatment.

El Salvador could be like that too.

You just never knew.

---

*   Which we were.

The Red Ghost, Miguel Marmol

IN HIS LAST MONTHS, Miguel Marmol, a hell-roaring communist revolutionary icon and among the last of his kind, sat in his niece's parlor in San Salvador and recalled being marched from prison to a truck with 17 other leftists and driven to the edge of the lakeside town of Ilopango to face a firing squad.

It was 1932, and the military government of Gen. Hernández Martínez had just crushed a peasant uprising of jobless indigenous Salvadorans who had had enough and whose *rara avis* democratically-elected government had been jerked out from under them.

The poor folks lost, the rich folks won, and for the government, it was payback time.

Marmol, a shoemaker, fisherman, union leader, peasant organizer, and founding member of El Salvador's Communist Party was born in 1905, on the Fourth of July, he wryly noted, out of wedlock and into the grinding poverty and hunger too common to the time and place.

He went to work early, mucking out the barracks at a National Guard base, and became a soldier at age 13. Biographers say one of his first missions was to help quell a relatively mild civilian and military uprising, and that the repression and torture he saw led him to seek a discharge and changed his life.

One night in 1918, a strong earthquake collapsed Marmol's barracks, killing many of the occupants. He had just left the barracks and narrowly missed being inside.

Such escapes became part and parcel of his legend.

The 1932 plot is considered the first avowedly communist-led uprising in Latin America. It was fueled by a worldwide depression, plunging coffee and sugar prices, joblessness, and an aristocracy infamously unfriendly to the desperately poor rural majority. It was also the first major armed revolt in El Salvador since a peasant rebellion had been quashed a century earlier.

Hernández's men killed everyone they could find whom they suspected of being a leftist, or anyone who looked like an Indian. El Salvador's indigenous population never really recovered from that.

But for the ham-handed firing squad, Marmol likely would have been just another forgotten victim of *la matanza,* the slaughter, that killed up to 30,000 people, mostly indigenous, in reprisal for the aborted revolt.

Instead he emerged from the bullets as a crown jewel of El Salvador's left.

In a 1992 interview the old rebel recalled the Mauser bullets pounding into him, falling wounded to the ground, laying stone-still in his blood and another man's gore, then telling police what they could do with themselves as they tried to stand him up to be shot again.

He remembered lying motionless covered with the brains of a Russian or a Pole who died at his side, while his captors discussed a coup de grace. They decided to leave Marmol for dead. He lived on to bedevil a string of military dictatorships for another 50 years.

In the modest home at the edge of San Salvador's General Cemetery, Marmol, then 88, remembered the night.

"There was the most beautiful moon," he said. The police had left the victims to the gravediggers. He crawled off into the darkness.

Miguel Marmol, circa 1966. Photo unknown.

He was among about 30 leftists who founded the country's Communist Party at Ilopango on the edge of San Salvador in 1930. In his autobiography, as told to guerrilla poet Roque Dalton in 1966, he recalled other details about the incident and the 15 nervous riflemen.* It took three volleys to bring down the first group, Marmol said. He and two others were in the second group.

"The commanding officer gave the order and the first round went over our heads. They didn't touch us and I thought they were just fucking around, to prolong the torture," he told Dalton.

---

* *Miguel Marmol*, which appeared in English in 1987 published by Curbstone Press.

Two more volleys barely grazed them. The captain cursed.

"With the fourth round they indeed wounded me, in the upper chest, but luckily it didn't go straight through but at an angle because of the way I turned when I heard the word 'Fire!' The bullet passed through my left nipple and arm.

"When some policeman from the firing squad came over to help me get up I was already on my feet again. 'Fuck it,' I said to them, 'You'll never put an end to us this way.'"

"I didn't think about the saints coming down from heaven or anything like that. My mother, yes, I thought of her. But more than anything, I don't know why, even there in that situation I felt that I was going to get out of that mess, that I wasn't going to die there. At any rate I collapsed, both feet kicking from the force of the impact."

"I don't know where the serenity, the feeling of invulnerability, came from," he says in the Dalton book. "Another round. Here, for sure, they hit me good. I felt several blows on my body and one like a sharp ring, like an electric shock going through my whole head. I was thinking clearly. The Russian's body was over mine and still dripping warm blood."

Two in the first group were still alive, Marmol recalled, and they cursed the policemen as they approached to finish them off.

"Then they came over to where I was stretched out. They lifted up the body of the Russian who showed no signs of life," he said.

"Later on I realized that a bullet that struck the Russian in the face had blown his brains out and some of the brain matter fell over my head, making it look like it was my brains coming out of the wounds on both my temples." He said they went through his pants but found (and took) only 80 centavos.

"For me centuries had passed and I felt like I had been reborn."

After he crawled away from where he was shot, friends treated him and found a nurse for him in a poor suburb of the capital.

"I told the nurse I had been hit by rocks," Marmol recalled in 1992. "But she said she knew what Mauser wounds looked like. She said I had to tell who I was or she would turn me over to the National Guard. I asked her if she believed in God and she said 'yes.' I told her, 'I am putting my life in your hands. I am Miguel Marmol.'"

"She told me, 'You are in the house of the bodyguard of Maximiliano Hernández.'" Friends got him out.

"From 1932 to 1934 the police, the National Guard, they called me 'The Red Ghost,'" he said with a chuckle. "They never could catch me. I had intuition. I knew in my dreams when they were coming to get me and when they got there, the Red Ghost was gone." He called his pursuers *los burlados,* the deceived ones.

He slid in and out of the country, to Guatemala, to Honduras, to Europe and the Soviet Union, sometimes for long periods, questioning, but never doubting his luck or his beliefs.

The 12-year Hernández regime set El Salvador on a course of nearly 50 years of military dictatorships and toward a ruinous civil war that shattered parts of the country.

In 1992, after the peace accords were signed, Marmol, recently back from 12 years of exile in Cuba, was still a proud member of the Communist Party, but inactive because of age.

An afternoon with Marmol evoked something trapped in amber, a hard-line remnant but not yet a relic, someone akin to a piney-woods torchlight evangelist in overalls, believing in something and little else, believing in it every inch of the way. No hemming here. No hawing.

Today's communists, he snarled, are a disgrace. "They aren't real revolutionaries anymore like we were," he said, leaning forward in a green metal lawn chair. "They're orthodox."

"I was leading strikes in February of 1921 when I was 16. Our youths were [spent] in the struggle. There were no sports for us, no movies, nothing but the progress of the movement.

"Farabundo Martí didn't know a wife or children. His lover was the struggle. I knew him well. He was a practical man, a dedicated revolutionary man. It was right out here, in the back of this house, where they executed him," he recalled that afternoon, gesturing toward the cemetery.

"We're not distorting our country's history when we say our Communist Party is the child of the Salvadoran working class since you won't find any instances, as occurred in other countries, where the CP was primarily organized in the university or among the petite bourgeois or intelligentsia," he was quoted as saying in the Dalton book.

"Our CP sprang from the very bowels of the working class."

Martí's name was adopted by the Farabundo Martí National Liberation Front. Hernández Martínez's name survived through the Maximiliano Hernández Martínez Brigade, the country's most notorious rightist death squad in the 1980s.

Marmol's name was not thus enshrined, but his legend grew as he played catch-me-if-you-can with authorities for years and worked as a party organizer.

He said in 1992 that he never had a real family. "I had three households over the years but never had the time to marry," he said slowly. His grandmother had tossed his unwed pregnant mother into the street in disgrace when she refused to name the father, and ran them both off again when she tried to return with the newborn Miguel.

A few discrepancies appear between the Dalton book and the 1992 interview, but that happens as legends are retold. The Dalton version has Marmol saying he faced the firing squad at night in the headlights of a truck, not on a sunny day. Dalton does not mention the bodyguard incident, a tale Marmol related with unalloyed gusto in 1992.

The old rebel referred to more than one wife when interviewed by Dalton. These were possibly "free union" relationships, often equated to marriage then and now.

Dalton cites Marmol as saying he nearly married his own sister because his father, something of a local bounder, had so many kids in the area nobody knew for sure who they were. Marmol also recalled nearly marrying a cousin.

All that aside, Marmol played a pivotal role in keeping alive the underpinnings of a revolutionary movement that blew wide open a half century later.

Like many of his comrades, he had spent years, even before he faced the firing squad, evading capture. Unlike them, he was alive at the end to tell the tale.*

Over decades, the world and leftist movements changed. Marmol never did.

Capitalism, he maintained in 1992, has never solved the problems of hunger and misery and was on its last legs. He defied a visitor to provide an example to the contrary.

---

* In 1975, the People's Revolutionary Army, to which Dalton adhered and which was a key part of the FMLN, accused Dalton of working against the organization and ordered him shot. They later admitted their mistake. Dalton was not quite 40. His biography *Miguel Marmol* is still the major biographical source.

Imperialism, he maintained, was the last gasp of capitalism, and imperialism was in full swing.

"Look at Peru. Look at Africa. The United States is in ruins."

He closed his eyes and leaned back, ticking off communist movements he had seen come and go. France. Spain. Italy. Eastern Europe.

"There's still China and, yes, Cuba, of course, and [North] Korea, and Vietnam…"

He tried to join the guerrilla fighters in the mountains of El Salvador in the early days of the war but the late Jorge Schafik Handal, the head of the military wing of the Salvadoran Communist Party Marmol helped found, told him he was too old.

At the party's insistence, he said, he slid out to Cuba through Nicaragua in 1980 and made frequent visits to Europe, Latin America, and, in 1988, to the United States to thump the tub for his cause.

"In 1988, 41 universities invited me to speak," he said. "I have the letters." His eyes brightened as he recalled selling kisses to co-eds after a speech at a university in Los Angeles.

He returned to El Salvador in August of 1992 along with wounded Salvadoran rebels who had been treated in Cuba.

The government and the FMLN fought a war of attrition more or less to a draw and actually signed a peace treaty, rare in revolutions, where the winner often takes all. Marmol maintained to the end that the FMLN won.

"They disbanded the National Guard and the Treasury Police," he said, referring to two brutal elements of the Salvadoran security forces.

"With one fist we fight to take power!" An FMLN poster collected by the author in El Salvador.

"With the United States on top of it all there was no chance for a [rebel] military victory. What could 13,000 of us do against 62,000 of them armed and trained by the gringos?

"It was stupid of us to think that we could have won here like we did in Cuba and Nicaragua, with our rifles. The United States would never have let that happen. The only way left for us, the only way out, was negotiation.

"It looks good to me. The war was a phase, the military phase. Then came the diplomatic phase and now it is the political phase and that could be as hard as the war was."

On the street in his marginal neighborhood vendors still sold cigarettes and aspirin one at a time, reminder and remnant of the poverty that was at the root of the war.

Marmol often turned pensive that afternoon, his ample chin resting on his T-shirted chest, his eyes closed. His face had Asian features from his indigenous bloodlines. At least once, while out of the country, he was tagged as a suspected Japanese spy.

Then he would snap back, alert, leaning forward.

"I didn't lose my reason with my age," he said, "even when [the former Soviet Union] fell.

"People used to accuse me of being a witch or something like that because I escaped so often. Look, there was nothing like that. I had my serenity, my self-confidence. I escaped death many times.

"Do you know what? One of the firing squad, before they shot us, told me he thought I was a pretty nice fellow."

He said he hoped to update the Dalton version of his life before he died but never did.

"I'm no writer, it's taking time," he said. "There is so much to tell, so much to write about.

"And the struggle. The struggle must keep going."

* * *

Marmol died June 25, 1993, of pneumonia. He is buried in the cemetery in back of where he lived. Hundreds attended his funeral.

Pro-Búsqueda

IN THE EMBATTLED city of Chalatenango in El Salvador's troubled north, Magdalena Ramos recalled seeing tired, muddy soldiers slogging back down rural roads in 1982. They had been pursuing peasants in scorched-earth campaigns through the hills to remove suspected guerrilla sympathizers.

Peeking from cloth wrappings around the soldiers' chests or from the tops of their backpacks were the tiny heads of terrified infants the soldiers had picked up on their sweeps, possibly after killing the parents. Many were malnourished and screaming for their mothers. Many of the parents had been trying to reach safety in Honduras with their children.

The soldiers usually left the children with anyone who would accept them, and by July of that year as the campaign against campesinos in the north intensified, rumors circulated that the Salvadoran Red Cross in the city of Chalatenango was giving children away.

Some local women were inclined to take the children but feared that they would draw suspicion since the infants were presumed to be children of guerrillas.

Ramos said that even in the regions near the *guindas* (in which massive groups of civilians attempted to escape Salvadoran military sweeps on foot), most only had a vague idea of what was going on back in the hills. Smart civilians didn't ask.

In the mornings, she writes in her memoirs of those years, trucks carrying combat troops headed out and helicopters took

Children at a refugee camp.
Photo: Pat Hamilton.

off from Military Base No. 1. There were rumors of towns destroyed and residents massacred, she writes, but they were hard to confirm.

But nearly two decades after the end of the war, reports of missing children still dribbled into the simple San Salvador offices of the Asociación Pro-Búsqueda de Niños y Niñas Desaparecidos, or the Association to Locate Missing Children.* By late 2009 Pro-Búsqueda had taken in 836 *denuncias,* or complaints.

"Of these 341 have been resolved and 241 investigations have resulted in meetings with the missing children and family members," said Mario José Sánchez González, a Nicaraguan national who took over the agency in 2005. More families have been reunited since then.

"We still get 15–20 cases a year. We have resolved eight or ten this year alone," he said then.

"Of course the numbers do not take into account cases where no complaint was filed out of fear or because all the relatives were dead," he said.

The missing kids have turned up as far away as the United States, Italy, and Australia.

Some were last seen being loaded aboard military helicopters after bloody sweeps of areas considered rebel friendly. That included much of Chalatenango, an area heavy with tiny villages and subsistence farmers, many of them impoverished sharecroppers.

Some of the children were adopted; some were in effect sold to adoptive parents abroad. Others?

"Many have made homes through adoption. They changed their names after being told they were orphans," he said. But it is turning out that often, they were not orphans.

---

* www.probusqueda.org.sv

Some were raised on military bases and some were adopted locally. A few even found their way to college. Others doubtless wound up on the often mean, gang-troubled streets of the capital.

"In some cases the kids were killed [in the military sweeps]," Sánchez González said. "We have been involved in exhumations and DNA testing. There have been many cases of that."

Most of the missing children vanished in the war's early years, 1980–1984.

"In some cases kids haven't wanted to be reunited. They remember only fear and massacres in their former lives," Sánchez said.

"There are cases where the adoptive parents don't want them to meet their biological families," he said. "They were adopted very young and the paperwork was very irregular. The adoptions may have been legal but they were very irregular. There would be a signature of someone who was not a family member saying the child was an orphan when it was not true, and the child was taken."

At the time, he recounted, there was a network of soldiers, orphanages, and government functionaries who found people in other countries willing to pay in the range of $20,000 for "legal fees" to facilitate adoption. Hundreds of children are believed to have wound up in the United States, Europe, and elsewhere outside El Salvador.

Pro-Búsqueda was founded after parents became upset that the Truth Commission, formed as part of the 1992 peace accords, did not deal specifically with the missing children, instead lumping them together with other victims of the conflict.

This led the late Jesuit priest Rev. Jon Cortina and other members of the departmental human-rights commission in Chalatenango to join with parents of the missing children.

The first successes came in 1994 when they found five children who had been missing since the massive guinda of May 1982, when more than 50 children vanished. Pro-Búsqueda said 15 eventually were located.

Many were taken to an orphanage, Aldeas Infantiles SOS, in Santa Tecla near San Salvador. They were reunited with their families in January of 1994.

That gave hope to other families, Cortina said, but they got no help from the ultra-conservative ARENA party in power at the time, so they formed Pro-Búsqueda that summer.

It took years after the peace deal was signed, but at least two books then emerged. One, *El día más esperado,* or "The Most-Awaited Day," examines the phenomenon from the point of view of the parents and other relatives who had children taken or otherwise lost in the panic and confusion of the times.

The other, *Historias para tener presente*[*], or roughly, "Stories to Keep Over Time" reconstructs those years through the eyes of the children, some of whom were very young when they were sucked up in the war and relied on the memories of older children in similar circumstances to fill some gaps. The family stories in the two books sometimes overlap.

They're adults now, but some of the missing still try to find family back in El Salvador or are sought by their Salvadoran relatives.

---

[*] *Historias para tener presente* and *El día más esperado* (both in Spanish), Editores UCA, Universidad Centroamericana José Simeón Cañas, San Salvador. www.ucaeditores.com.sv

The Inter-American Human Rights Court and other judicial organizations have since ordered the Salvadoran government to investigate specific cases and to form a commission to find the children and create a DNA bank.

President Mauricio Funes, elected on the now center-left Farabundo Martí National Liberation Front ticket in March of 2009, said in early 2010 that such a commission would be formed, and it was functioning in 2011.

Pro-Búsqueda says it believes about 90 percent of the cases of missing children can be blamed on the military and about 10 percent on the FMLN, very roughly on par with levels of blame for war crimes laid down by the U.N. Truth Commission.

Andrea Dubon was seven when she lost her left arm to shrapnel from an aerial bombing during the May 1982 guinda. That and other wounds prevented her from walking or standing.

Her father made the heartbreaking choice of leaving her on the edge of a canyon as government troops approached and he and the rest of the family plunged over the edge to save any among them they could, she recalled in *Historias para tener presente*.

Soldiers took her to the Red Cross in the city of Chalatenango and she eventually wound up at Aldeas in Santa Tecla. The international nonprofit aids abandoned and orphaned children and vastly expanded its Salvadoran operations during the war. It has worked in scores of countries.

She related how her father had bundled her across his chest with a cloth as the family fled advancing troops, hiding in hand-dug caves, or *tatues,* during the day, moving at night to avoid detection, foraging for fruit, always hungry.

But at the edge of a large gully, the helicopters arrived. Some of those on the run plunged over the edge, she said, but she learned from her father ten years later that he believed that if he went over the edge with her and with her sister all three would be caught and killed.

"At that moment my father decided to leave me," she wrote. "He untied me from his breast, gave me a last kiss, laid me under a tree at the edge of the gulch and jumped into it with my sister in his arms."

She said later that she can't blame him, because "it was a choice no human being should ever see himself forced to make."

She told of mothers forced to stuff rags in the mouths of infant children, suffocating them so their crying would not give away the hiding places to the soldiers.

Others told of children being forced by soldiers to call for their mothers, only to see "big papayas," or mortar shells, fall on the locations of the parents who answered, then hearing the parents' screams.

She said the soldiers took her and some other children to the Red Cross in Chalatenango. From there they went by ambulance to Aldeas, where she remained for more than ten years, always, she said, wondering if her family had survived.

When she arrived, she recalled, she remembered little of the day the bombs fell on the village where she lived with her parents and five siblings.

"I have no memories but I have souvenirs," she wrote much later.

They included a missing left arm and a young body full of crippling shrapnel.

Much of what she learned about her last days in the countryside came from others who were there or from adults she contacted much later.

She did remember fleeing, horribly wounded, with her family when the bombs began falling.

It wasn't the first time they fled the soldiers, but the previous retreats had lasted just a week or two, "and later our families were able to return to set themselves up somewhere. Not this time. The army began a persecution that never stopped."

At Aldeas she recalled getting schooling, medical care, physical therapy, and surgery to correct the injuries, and eventually being sent to college to become a social worker. She recalled being selected as one of the Aldeas children to greet Pope John Paul II at the San Salvador airport when he visited the country as a part of a Central American tour in 1983.

But she and others there were given no hope that their parents might have survived. Hers, as it turned out, did, escaping to a refugee camp in Honduras. But at the time, who knew?

The other kids at Aldeas had the same concerns but didn't discuss them when adults were present, she recalled.

When they were alone, things were different.

"We entered a prohibited topic, something it was 'best not to talk about,'" she wrote in her recollections.

"The adults always intimidated us with this: 'Don't talk about what happened, it will hurt you even more. Don't think about your family. They're guerrillas, they're dead.'"

However, she said the classification of "orphan" weighed heavily on her and others at Aldeas, and there was no evidence ever presented that their parents were in fact dead.

Those who tell their stories in the two books make it clear that materiel and other support for the guerrillas ran high in the affected regions, due at least in part to long-standing abuses by government troops and landowners that began well before the war got going.

The government policy then was described as "taking the water away from the fish," or removing the atmosphere in which rebel forces could easily operate.

As stories, rumors, and reports of sightings of possible family members circulated in a very small country and searches began, Dubon discovered that her parents were very much alive. She was reunited with them in 1994, 12 years after she had seen them last.

Meanwhile Andrea had been assigned a new last name and birthday and had gone through school.

She told of the "volunteer ladies" who would arrive at Aldeas to try to remove the children and put them up for adoption, a plan foiled by Aldeas workers who locked the children away and called authorities, lending credence to claims that a bootleg adoption network was a thriving concern.

Then word came to her in early 1994 that a young man in jeans and cowboy boots claiming to be her cousin had come to Aldeas looking for her. A short time later the Aldeas director told her that her parents and relatives of a few other kids there had been found alive in Chalatenango. Did she want contact with them?

Aldeas had gotten word of the likelihood two weeks earlier when a pickup full of then-unidentified peasants visited from Chalatenango, but they kept it secret while they investigated. The next day they all headed to the isolated Chalatenango village of Guarjila for emotional reunions they had come to believe would never take place.

Other kids were raised on military bases and recalled being generally well treated and educated. In May of 1980, two brothers, then eight and five, had seen their mother and an infant sibling shot before their eyes. They and hundreds of others were fleeing to the Sumpul River and Honduras, the scene of one of the war's worst massacres. Soldiers on both sides of the river shot at the fleeing peasants and may have killed 300 or more.

Things had been somewhat unstable along the border river, especially since a four-day border war in 1969 that claimed about 4,000 lives on each side. Honduras was getting edgy over the increasing number of refugees who might be rebel sympathizers crossing from El Salvador.

The brothers, Mauricio and Almicar Guardado, had been across the river before when their family sought refuge and found a welcome of sorts among the peasants there.

Suddenly Honduran troops appeared telling them they had 24 hours to go back to El Salvador, and stood guard to make sure they did so.

Later they and hundreds of others had to flee again, hoping to cross the rain-swollen river back to Honduras. Salvadoran troops fired at them as they fled, and Honduran soldiers did so as they approached the other side.

The brothers were put aboard a helicopter and taken to the main air force base at Ilopango, where they were schooled and raised.

They said they eventually made friends there but were treated at times as curiosities, encouraged by officers, for small coins or pieces of fruit, to sing what they could remember of rebel songs they knew from infancy.

They recalled generally getting on well, even with some of the wounded soldiers, but not with all of them. One, they said, falsely accused them of stealing a towel and told them if he had been on the Sumpul operation he wouldn't have left them alive.

They told him, they recalled, that if they had been guerrillas, they wouldn't have let him escape either.

It is hard to imagine that anybody smiled.

The brothers said they quickly learned that there were two kinds of Salvadoran soldiers: ordinary troops just trying to survive who would not harm unarmed civilians, and psychopaths who made cruelty a cherished part of their jobs.

While those years are properly defined in most minds by horror and death, the U.N. Truth Commission report, highly critical of the Salvadoran military, also makes multiple references to soldiers who refused orders to kill civilians.

Another lost child, Lucio, whose last name is not given, wrote of being on the run off and on for years with his father, who sometimes carried him on his shoulders or in a jute bag over his back when the boy was too exhausted to continue.

He remembered his mother being taken away by soldiers to be tortured and shot when he was not quite four years old and abandoning the house with his father, probably in 1981. He figured his father was about 50, and helped out the rebels from time to time but was considered too old for combat.

He said his father recalled how neighbors said they knew the soldiers were going to kill his mother by the manner in which they took her away.

"They led her rather far away," Lucio said, "They tortured her, wounding her all over her body, they abused her sexually and burned her with acid before delivering the two final shots. In the house we heard only the shots."

When his father heard of it and went to investigate, he said, he only had time for a partial on-the-spot burial before the bullets flew again.

Some months later, he said, word came that soldiers were returning to the area and that they were told to meet at the Peñas Ranch because it was a major military operation.

While awaiting the word to move out they heard the first shots.

He said many people died there, "maybe hundreds." He said they fled for several days. "I don't remember how many, but it seemed an eternity. We would walk for awhile then hide. There would be someone who would climb a tree or a rock to see if soldiers were coming near. If they were then we would run again. This guinda was tough."

He said his father told him they had to stay on the Chichontepec volcano, home and hideout to them and many others, where Lucio was born, because if they went down below they would be recognized and singled out.

"But I believe the main reason my father had to stay on the volcano was the death of my mother; he felt he could not go without getting revenge."

His father eventually was killed by a mine. As he was dying, Lucio recalled, his father told him someone would come for him and made him promise to get out of the region and go to school.

Someone came. Lucio boarded a bus, the first time he had ever done so, and arrived in Soyapango near the capital, where the lady who came for him introduced him to her mother. For the first time in his life he slept on a mattress. He was nine.

He was told not to mention comrades or guerrillas or the FMLN because the area was crawling with *orejas* (ears), government snitches, and he would quickly be singled out.

Later, he recalled, he was sent to the house of a lawyer who had three cars and servants. And there were toys. His favorite, he recalled, was a plastic submachine gun that made a noise when you pulled the trigger.

From there it was to a series of orphanages, some, he recalled, quite abusive, and eventually through Pro-Búsqueda, to a reunion with what remained of his family.

There were times when parents took the painful step of giving up their children out of fear for their future or an inability to care for them in wartime.

For nearly two decades Martina Torresendi lived the life of a normal Italian, raised as an only child. She knew she had been adopted from distant El Salvador but knew little else until 2003, when she got a telephone call from a woman claiming to be her sister, living nearby in Rome.

"I have a wonderful family in Italy and that always was enough," said Martina, then 28. Still, she said she often had dreamt that she had a sibling.

The two got together She and her sister Silvia rejoiced at length, noting physical resemblances, catching up as sisters will.

How, they wondered, could they have been raised in the same country for so many years, displaced by the same distant war, each unaware the other was there?

Martina went back to El Salvador in December of 2009 for another emotional meeting, this time with her biological mother.

When the two met at Pro-Búsqueda, her mother, Graciela, told BBC Mundo, the British Broadcasting Corp's Spanish service, that she "felt as if an angel had arrived from on high."

Then the stories rolled out.

Graciela had not seen Martina, baptized Janet Ruiz, since the girl was 18 months old in 1982, when the war was roaring.

A year earlier the family had been displaced in the troubled east by guerrillas, who had killed Martina's father. Graciela found herself alone with four small children and nowhere to turn.

Her brother said he knew of a lawyer who could help. She wouldn't hear of it at first but finally accepted. "It was fear and uncertainty that convinced me," she said. "That and the bombs."

They went to the capital to meet the lawyer and one of the Italian families at a luxury hotel where Graciela said goodbye to her daughters.

The lawyer said the adoptive parents would bring the girls back for a visit every seven years and send photos each year, but after a year and a half there was no further word.

The sisters were among those found by Pro-Búsqueda.

Pro-Búsqueda lawyer Leonor Arteaga wrote that in those years there were lawyers who routinely prowled refugee camps and areas where people gathered looking for children eligible for adoption.

While Martina insisted her adoptive parents "didn't pay for me," she said she believed many others did and agreed that many adoptions happened without the parents knowing the truth about the children's status.

Lucía Panameño, who was 70 in late 2009, told BBC Mundo she still can't explain how her granddaughter came to be living thousands of miles away in the United States.

She lives now in the department of San Vicente where she last saw the girl in 1982.

Her granddaughter was wounded while the family fled a military offensive and she became separated in the confusion.

A judge later classified her as "abandoned."

"Maybe she will come back some day at least once to see us," the grandmother said sadly. The girl's parents are dead and the last Lucía knew the girl was in Virginia.

Pro-Búsqueda psychologist Alexis Rivas, said many adopted children living out of the country have not come back to seek blood relatives.

"They have their own families, they may be afraid of losing what they have or be angry because they think they were given away," he said.

Such children, now grown, have an outlook on the war few can share or appreciate.

"It bothers me when people fought just to live. It bothers me when they have such a simplistic idea of the war, when they contend that the guerrillas just came to destroy the country and things such as that," said Armando, who was sent to Aldeas after his mother was killed and remembered the arrival there of the little girl with only one arm.

"The war was difficult, unjust, maybe crazy, but above all it was painful. I think about my mother and how she met her end. All I ask is a little respect for her and for all of the huge emptiness it has left in our lives."

The children whose sagas are recorded in the book agreed, and an epilogue, apparently written jointly, speaks volumes.

"The most incredible thing about our stories is that we are alive to tell them," they wrote in the epilogue to *Historias*. "Sadly, many of our family members didn't have the good fortune to save themselves."

"There is almost no documentation and very little information about the massacre at Sumpul [River] and about the military operations in Cabañas and Chalatenango. If we had not been able to ask our relatives who also survived what happened, we probably never would have known the truth.

"The mass media said the armed forces won this or that objective but never talked about the outrages and massacres they committed to make it happen. If something about that appeared in some newspaper in those years it was expressed in terms of 'terrorist delinquents'…

"We hope that through out narratives it is clear that that does not reflect in any way what we or our families experienced.

"The war continues to be a hidden episode for most Salvadorans. Without knowing how it really was, some people say the war was the fault of one band or the other. Others think that, having been in the capital during the offensives, they know what war was.

"But they didn't live what the people in the countryside lived."

Cinquera: The War and Small Towns

ON A FRAYED and filthy straw mat where the besieged town of Cinquera faded into farmland, Mayor Cordelia Avalos de Hernández lay curled up on a curbside, sobbing. The pavement around her was littered with cartridge casings.

The last of the town's 5,000 or so remaining residents were streaming out to somewhere, anywhere, with help from the military. What was left would soon be bombed to near oblivion, and would remain empty for eight years.

It was May of 1983 in the market town just 45 miles northeast of the capital. What happened here was typical of what happened in dozens of rural villages out of sight, out of mind and out of touch with much of the rest of El Salvador, even more so with the larger world.

"I lost everything. They robbed everything and they were going to kill me," mumbled Avalos, then 56, her eyes glazed. She said the rebels looted her small grocery store.

"I have two grandsons, they have no mother or father. The guerrillas killed their mother a year ago and I have to support them now. I know how to sew a little."

Things got ugly in Cinquera during a local feud in 1980 when a dissident priest led many of the town's leftist sympathizers into the hills to join the guerrillas.

Remaining townspeople, many of whom leaned right, claimed about 30 government troops were killed trying to take the rebel-held town back. They said ten people who surrendered were executed including several rightists pulled from their homes by guerrillas identified as among those who joined the rebels with the priest.

Carrying water in rural El Salvador.
Photo: Pat Hamilton.

People began filtering back in February of 1991, including Pablo Albarengo Escobar, a lifelong resident known to everyone as "Lolo." He said there wasn't a house standing.

"It was a jungle," he said in 2009 in the living room of his modest home, which doubles as a hole-in-the-wall grocery store with splotched white walls and a cracked concrete floor.

Pictures of revolutionary heroes gaze down at visitors. Castro, Che Guevara, Farabundo Martí. Another wall is covered with war relics—a battered military canteen, a cartridge belt, a rusted-out G-3 assault rifle, the kind used by the National Guard.

On a wall outside is an honor role of sorts with the names of area people who died fighting government forces. It is a long list for a small town.

"When [the air force] would bomb Chalatenango they would always leave us a little gift. They always saved four or five bombs for Cinquera. They dropped them every day. Everything you see here is new. Trees were growing up from the rubble of the houses. People cut them down with axes," Lolo, then 70, said.

He said most of those who returned in 1991 supported the guerrilla forces.

The war put Salvadorans on the move by the hundreds of thousands—to relatives' homes, out of the country, or, more often, to filthy refugee camps and makeshift cardboard shantytowns along abandoned railway lines.

"We came back and tried to live a normal life. But the bombings continued for months after that. The first thing we did was to build trenches in the town to protect us from the shrapnel," Lolo said.

A few of the 500- or 750-pound government bombs were duds, and townspeople dug them out and stripped them of their explosives, not a job for the squeamish.

Three of the steel bombshells sat in front of the partially rebuilt church in 2011.

When the National Guard left Cinquera they took the bronze church bell, he said, probably to sell it for scrap. The town couldn't afford to replace it, so someone bangs on the empty bomb casings with a rock to call a town meeting.

And the mayor sobbing on the straw mat?

"She was our adversary, she worked with those against us," he said bitterly. "There were a lot of deaths because of that woman. She has many things pending with the people here. She denounced many people who were killed by the military."

He said he thought she fled to the mostly conservative nearby town of Ilobasco. He didn't know where she ended up. He wanted to.

Cinquera and towns like it are scattered along rough roads leading into dry hills, places people who don't live there seldom see.

Lolo too fled, and spent some time working with people displaced by the fighting in a filthy refugee camp behind the rather stately former headquarters of the Archbishop of San Salvador in the capital, a building since turned into a seminary.

Tiny, isolated towns, some with only a few hundred residents, suffered every ugly aspect of the war. Those who did not flee to the relative safety of the capital or try to leave the country altogether hovered at the war's edge—and at its mercy.

The small towns saw much of the worst of the war and often they saw it alone.

Soldiers of the American-trained elite Atlacatl Battalion entered the village of El Mozote in the rebel-run department of Morazán on December 10, 1981, and began the most infamous massacre of the war, killing everyone they could find. Estimates vary widely, from "more than 200" to more than 1,000 men, women, and children.

Joseph Frazier

For years the common belief was that there were only two survivors, but groups dedicated to reuniting missing children with relatives now say several children were taken from El Mozote by soldiers and delivered to orphanages, and that some have been reunited with their families. A few adults who survived the killings in the villages around El Mozote have also come forward.

"They killed a few of us that night but it was on the 11th, the next morning, that the real massacre took place," survivor Rufina Amaya, who has since died, recalled in a 1993 interview with the AP in nearby Segundo Montes, where she worked with a Christian women's group. She had told the tale often.

"They closed us up in houses and in the morning they brought people out in groups to be killed," she said. "First the fathers, then the mothers, then the children."

She said she had crawled behind some pineapple plants and had to watch as her husband and four children were shot. "From where I was hiding I could hear them cry and scream," she said.

When friends found her, lost and dazed days later in the hills, most of her clothing had been torn off by brush and thorns.

"Before God, I have told the truth about what happened," she said. "Sometimes I get down on my knees and ask Him to take me away from the memories."

The United States and El Salvador at first denied everything after it was initially reported by Ray Bonner of the *New York Times* and Alma Guillermoprieto of the *Washington Post*, who visited the site at some risk shortly after the killings took place.

Writer Mark Danner in the *New Yorker* may have pegged what El Mozote stood for beyond the lives lost. He said it became known and was allowed to fall back in the dark. "How it came to be known and how it came to be denied was a central parable of the Cold War."

The Atlacatl Battalion was disbanded in 1992 as a part of the peace accords. In 1984, its commander, Col. Domingo Monterrosa, a diminutive, shy-looking man, was killed when troops loaded what they thought was captured rebel radio gear on his helicopter not far from El Mozote. It contained a bomb, which the guerrillas set off by remote control, killing all on board.

Monterrosa was adored by his troops. As he met with them to send them on furlough after a long operation in Morazán in 1983, two soldiers, one with a guitar, sang a song they had written in his honor.

He bade them farewell with fatherly advice: do what you want at home but not in uniform.

"You can buy a tonel [keg] of brandy and lie under it and let it drip down your throat all night if you want," he said licking his lips and swallowing as an example.

"Verga, verga," came the responses, an uber-ribald equivalent of "far out!"

They asked permission to fire a salute in his honor.

"Solo dos, solo dos," he told them as he paced up and down in front of the soldiers. "Only two rounds each." A hundred or so M-16s pointed upward blew off easily 40 rounds each in a few seconds.[*]

What else went on down rural roads was cause for speculation, but as the war progressed etchings of wartime life in rural El Salvador emerged.

In 1983, Tenancingo, 30 miles east of the capital, was a town of dirt streets, dingy stucco-covered adobe buildings

---

[*] What went up did come down, and later in the day townspeople reportedly complained of pock-marked cars. But they did so quietly. In those years small rural towns were bad places to get crosswise with the military, doubly so with the Atlacatl.

speckled with bullet holes, no electricity, and no running water.

For some, there was no way out.

Angela María Casseres leaned against a smudged glass counter of her tiny grocery sore, watching as a guerrilla loaded supplies on a swayback horse preparing to return to the mountains.

They paid for what they took, she said, but they set the price.

"I have 14 children. I can't move from here because I don't have the 100 colones [then about $40] it would cost me to rent somewhere else. The kids ask for more to eat but I can't leave. They have the flu and there is no medicine for them here."

Outside, Spanish slogans covered the walls.

"Soldier, surrender and we will guarantee your lives."—"Yanquis in El Salvador will bite the dust of defeat."—"Viva Cuba."—"Fuck America."

The other side had been there too. "The Popular Liberation Forces are nothing but pigs," read one scrawled message.

All that remained on Casseres's shelves was one egg, one flashlight battery, about four pounds of beans, some sugar, and some salt.

A week or so earlier guerrillas had routed the army garrison and the government choked off most food deliveries to keep them from falling into rebel hands.

When food came, such as it was, the Red Cross delivered it.

"They only let them bring in two arobas [about 50 pounds] of salt yesterday," she said.

Tenancingo once had about 12,000 residents, but shrunk to about 5,000 soon after the army fled. Residents said even half of those had left in recent days.

"The ones who stayed are those with no way to leave," Casseres said.

At the time the left controlled about ten percent of the towns in the country and was beginning to sniff victory. In some areas demoralized government troops dropped their guns and fled.

An American military advisor said at about that time that he believed the Salvadoran government had maybe six months to turn the thing around "or they could lose it."

One of the guerrillas in Tenancingo, who gave his name as Santos, said he was 18 and had been with the Popular Liberation Forces for five years, not unusual for the time and place.

He turned and waved as he and two comrades led the loaded horse down the rough street past scrawny dogs and a few kids, but no adult males.

The kids eagerly volunteered to take visitors to where the fighting was heaviest.

Tenancingo, too, was soon all but abandoned.

By 1986 a few residents were back, hoping both sides would honor a pledge brokered by the Roman Catholic Church and the International Red Cross not to make it a target again.

City hall was but a shell, houses were burned out and bullet holes pocked the walls, some of which were smeared with what looked a lot like dried blood.

Paper banners proclaiming "Welcome people back to Tenancingo" were signed by the FMLN.

A pickup loaded with wooden images of saints inched through ankle-deep dust toward the church, much of which had been lost to bombs and scavengers.

Guerrillas had attacked the town in September of 1983, trapping a military garrison. Government bombs nearly leveled the town and killed some 50 civilians, an air strike the government later said was unauthorized.

Out in the east, in La Sociedad, more often than not a rebel stronghold, young women sat on a store porch in early 1982 waiting to fill jugs from the only source of running water in the town.

The only men were old. And the others?

"They went to the capital to work," said one.

"What kind of work?"

"A job."

"Doing what?"

"Working."

This was not discussed further. They were in the hills with rebel forces and everyone knew that everyone knew it.

It was the same story to the south, where the Puente de Oro, or Golden Bridge, once a major east-west link, lay in the Lempa River like a snake with a broken back. "The boys" had blown it up to celebrate the second anniversary of the 1979 coup that helped get the war rolling.

A woman in a pink dress said rebel forces regularly moved through nearby San Marcos Lempa but didn't bother people.

For the past three weeks she had been walking to the nearby town to try to collect wages for picking cotton, maybe $4 or $5 for a sunup to sundown day if she was lucky.

Each time, she said, she was told the money had somehow not arrived. She'd try again tomorrow.

San Marcos Lempa was full of women and kids. The men and boys?

"They went away. They're working somewhere else."

"Where?"

"Working."

It was the same in San Sebastián, a relatively well-off town 30 miles east of San Salvador, famed for the colorful cloth residents made on the large wooden looms that dominated their front rooms and courtyards. On a hot afternoon the *clack-clack-clack* of the shuttles was the only sound from the homes along the overgrown streets.

Normal activity had slowed to a crawl after three years of rebel attacks, but a government plan to train local militiamen and pay residents to repair the damage was bringing a few people back to what had become a ghost town.

Leonore Almelda Constanzia showed a visitor the bombed-out shell of her house.

"The house was all right when we left," she said, adding that rebuilding it would be difficult.

"But the climate is good here. And who can forget home?"

The mood was lighter up in Tejutepeque, where a couple of weeks before Christmas children carrying images of Joseph and Mary paraded through town in a traditional Posada ceremony, reciting the centuries-old plea from house to house: "In the name of heaven we ask lodging, my beloved wife cannot continue."

"This is not an inn, be away with you," sang those inside as their part of the traditional back-and-forth, until they finally responded, "Well, enter, then." Refreshments were served.

Out in the town square, a rebel musical group, the Farabundo Trillo, belted out their own message in mariachi-style songs.

"Fight with courage and we will give you a piece of land when it is distributed," they sang. "President Reagan is so worried about losing the war that all his hair will fall out."

From the children across the square: "The fishes in the water rejoiced when the Baby Jesus was born."

There were a few aluminum or paper decorations. A bread vendor said a well-meaning native who had moved to the capital had brought strings of colored electric lights as a gift the town.

"We haven't had electricity here in two years," the vendor shrugged.

"They're in charge, aren't they?" asked a resident as he watched the rebels and children. "And look, there isn't much entertainment around here these days."

Generally small-town residents who couldn't get away or chose to stay for a variety of reasons just tried to adapt.

In 1983, in the village of Concepción Quetzaltepeque, one of about 20 towns in the northern department of Chalatenango where they came and went at will, guerrillas of the Popular Liberation Forces held a big meeting with the townspeople. A town official said about 400 rebels strolled into the town. "They came from all sides, at about six in the morning and there were women and kids with them," said a local official who like most in similar situations, declined to give his name.

"They held a two-hour meeting in the square. They had a megaphone and they told the people they would win the war and that they should not be manipulated by the Americans. Then at about 2 p.m. they strolled back into the hills."

He said they wanted food but didn't steal. "I suppose some people gave them things voluntarily," he said.

In nearby Dulce Nombre de María (Sweet Name of Mary) a justice of the peace said rebel forces went through there constantly with no government opposition. Asked how many and how often, he shrugged. "Well, most people here go to bed pretty early at night so maybe they don't see too much."

The next day the town's eight-piece band and a group of masked clowns led merry-makers down the cobbled main street.

A elderly woman who owned a one-table restaurant on the plaza said to an inquiring reporter as she watched the clowns, "What do I think of the guerrillas coming here? I don't think at all. See the clown with the death's mask head? That's in honor of San Sebastián. He was a martyr, you know."

In areas where fighting was heavier many small-town residents with no choice fled to the often-crude refugee camps that popped up across the country. It was here that the pathos flowed.

Many were sick or had lost family members to disease or murder. Few had anyplace else to go or anybody to help them get there.

Often, camps set up for pro-government refugees fleeing the fighting weren't all bad.

At a camp run by the pro-government Salvadoran National Red Cross, about 450 people fleeing rebel activity lived in a school with a playground. Doctors visited regularly with ample medicine. Food seemed plentiful and kids played lively soccer and basketball games. Up the hill an army post kept a weather eye open.

Balbino Anaya, who was 66 in 1981, said it was the rebels who threatened and killed people in the Cuscatlán area where he lived.

"They would kill the boys who refused to join them and they wouldn't let us do anything. They didn't want the harvest brought in."

He said he brought his family to the center when rebels shot to death seven people he was working with in a field.

It was a different story back in the capital, behind the archbishop's headquarters, where Lolo (Albarengo Escobar) had left his home town of Cinquera and worked with some 1,000 refugees who also had fled government troops.

"Do you see that dust in the wind?" he asked in 1981. "We eat that dust in our food. This is an unhealthy place."

"There is sickness and there is not enough water," he said. "Some children die. They have no papers and we bury them where we can. We buried a pregnant woman over here."

Lolo said medical students sometimes visited but that doctors rarely did for fear of reprisals.

Most residents were women, children, and the elderly. Lolo readily conceded that the missing young men may well have been in the hills with the rebels.

Bitterness was as thick as the smoke from the cooking fires in the camp.

"The National Guard came and burned our house," said Marta Romero, 24, who had arrived three months earlier with her five children.

"They took away my husband because he was spreading the word of God. They took him away when they burned our house. I know nothing of him since then."

Helena Rodríguez, from the troubled department of San Vicente, said soldiers came to her small village and burned the houses of everybody except those of ORDEN families.

ORDEN, or the National Democratic Organization, was formed with the help of the United States in the 1960s to help keep tabs on rural leftist activity.

Officially it was dissolved in 1979, but it lived on in the paramilitary Civil Guard that operated in many towns.

Back at the pro-government camp a woman boiling beans over an outdoor fire didn't look up and didn't give her name.

"Los malos [the bad ones], they kept coming. Everyone in my village was afraid. Plenty of them came here."

She said she was harvesting coffee on a nearby plantation when the guerrillas opened fire.

"I didn't see them," she said, nursing an infant and feeding more sticks into the fire.

"I was working. No, I saw nothing. I saw nothing at all."

La Libertad and Surfer Bob

At Punta Roca, a breezy seafront bar and restaurant, something whispered of another time, far from the civil war that surrounded it. It was perhaps a 45-minute drive from the often-tense wartime capital, but it felt light-years away.

Punta Roca was proudly without pretense, with an almost arrogant and in-your-face attitude toward pricier (but rarely better) watering holes and the class differences that helped define the country and stoke its war.

There is an old-time, low-key calm about Punta Roca and its town of La Libertad, like something from a faded watercolor.

Quietly at the helm was, and is, Bob Rotherham, the quintessential former surf bum turned entrepreneur-raconteur-adventurer-businessman, an ex-pat Floridian who stopped off during a surfing trip to Panama in 1972 to check the waves. He never left and says he never plans to. Neither would you.

While many fled El Salvador's civil war and its horrors, Rotherham lived it and stayed the course.

"I lived through the civil war here," he said, relaxing on the patio of his restaurant. "I missed the Vietnam draft lottery by one number. I had my own civil war here."

"Surfer Bob" held sway in Punta Roca's shadows during the war as an eclectic flow of people—journalists, military men, a guerrilla leader's wife, a military chopper pilot, probable spies and snitches, just about everybody—paused for an hour or two if they could find it.

Think back to the movie *Casablanca,* with Humphrey Bogart and the catch-all café and bar called Rick's Café Americain.

Add surf, sun, a humid breeze. There was no casino, but people minded their own business. That was Punta Roca.

"The wife of [People's Revolutionary Army leader] Joaquín Villalobos was a customer, she used to come here," Rotherham said.

So did middle-aged Salvadorans with military haircuts, some of whom once dressed down an itinerant busker for singing mild protest songs while he trolled for stray coins. They asked the busker what subversive group he belonged to. He left.[*]

Everybody filtered through the simple tables, cheap shrimp and conch cocktails, and very cold beer—freelance mariachis seriously in need of tune-ups, chunks of the foreign press corps who could scrounge some time, child vendors of raw cashews and seashell necklaces, shoe-shiners, cripples seeking handouts, sons of the well-shod, and people who could be anybody. It somehow seemed prudent not to ask. So far as we could tell, diplomats avoided the place. In its way it was a tiny Times Square, where it is said that if you wait long enough in one place the person you seek will show up.

During the war we approached Rotherham from time to time to see how he did his balancing act through the opposing pressures, but he tended to turn his back. He wasn't being hostile. Bob was just prudent. With the war long over, he spent a casual afternoon in late 2009 discussing the more delicate times, pre-war dictatorships, his love of the place,

---

[*] A few of us shanghaied the busker later and got him to a hotel room in the capital where he performed for a hastily assembled group of TV cameramen and sound technicians. The videotape is out there somewhere. He was quite good.

surfing (naturally), the delights of corruption (in a nice way, of course) and, in general, survivorship.

"I still surf all the time," he said at age 60. "It keeps me going. I hold my own in the competitions. And I could tell you a million stories about this place."

So he began.

"Before the war this place had lots of characters, La Libertad has always been a magnet for characters. A lot of them could have come out of Zap Comix, names like Zippy Pinhead and Brown Dog. It was out of the movies.

"There was a girl who went by the name of Woodstock. She used to service all of the surfers, 10 or 15 at a time."

Surfing, he said, put El Salvador on the tourism map in the mid-70s and is driving the country's push to reestablish a tourism industry today.

"Then when the war came the surfers started to clear out," he said. "A few stayed around because there was good water and there was nobody out there."

But he said the scene is changing.

"Now we get Internet surfers, they don't care what they pay. They zero in on the waves from March to November. They get world wave and weather reports and hit it on the head when the swells will be the best."

While the earlier batch might stay around and get to know area residents, he said, the newer crowd might go to their hotel, hit the waves, and leave in a couple of days.

"They might not even go to the dock down there," he said, pointing to a pier that juts into the ocean and where small fishing dories are lowered and raised by crane, where fresh seafood is sold by fishermen's families.

"There are perfect waves for surfing at nine points within about a mile and a half of the port. Many are not for novices but they are fine for people with mediocre experience. They are not extreme."

A few middle-aged diehards, he said, still stay longer and mix with the community.

"But back then we got surfers from Texas, Australia, lots of spaced-out Brazilians. We had a postmaster who would feel the arriving letters for contraband [drugs] and set them aside. You were supposed to tip him a few colons."

Then as now in El Salvador, he recalled, money and family could do wonders. "You can use corruption to your advantage. But you don't want corruption to come after you," he said.

During the military dictatorship of Gen. Arturo Molina (1972–1977), he recalled, there was a lavish party at a now-vanished hotel a few hundred yards south of Punta Roca along the beach.

"It was really something," he said. "Security was amazing. They stopped all of our cars and took us all in. Some people in the car had been smoking dope.

"A friend told the soldiers his name was Roberto Levy Molina Molina[*] and that he was going to see his uncle Arturo at the party.

"They snapped to attention. They even gave Roberto back his stash. Out of Zap Comix. Out of the movies."

It wasn't all skittles and suds.

In the very early 1980s, he recalled fondly, a National Assembly deputy was caught out after the 7 p.m. shoot-to-kill curfew.

"They could have shot him right there, and they might have, but he left his wallet on the car seat and somehow the soldiers recognized him.

---

[*] This much, Bob says, was true.

"He told them he was going to visit his old friend Roberto Rotherham at La Libertad. He was slobbering drunk. He had pissed his pants.

"So I look outside and here are all these jeeps and military vehicles and I thought, 'They're going to take us away.'"

"But there was Roberto, drunk as a skunk. They asked if I was responsible for this guy. He sobered up and stayed here three days."

And Rotherham got tastes of the war's rougher side.

When his kids were in a Catholic school in Santa Tecla, several miles inland, he recalled, he and his Salvadoran wife drove there to get their report cards.

"The school encouraged family involvement. Coming back we ran into a military roadblock. My wife said not to stop but I did. They pulled us out and drove our truck away.

"They threw us in a ditch. They were carrying cans of Colt 45 and they all were very drunk. They said they were going to kill us.

"Another said to hold off, we might be priests or nuns," apparently recalling the global outrage that followed the murders of three American nuns and a lay social worker by National Guard troops in 1980.

He said they took them to a brick building where soldiers were raping girls and women.

"They tried to separate my son Jimmy* from my wife. She clawed the soldier's face open. They took our wedding rings and billfolds."

He said they put them back in their vehicle for a time and that he remembered rifles being cocked.

---

* A world-ranked surfer.

"About midnight we decided we weren't just going to sit there, we would walk out. But we found they were gone."

He said they later found the truck in a ditch with the keys still in the ignition and recognized the man with the torn-up face as a radioman on an army tank.

"We have had good times and bad times," he said, blaming the latter mostly on "being in the wrong place at the wrong time."

Rotherham, balding now, with black-rimmed glasses and a grizzle of beard, says he has no regrets. He has opened a hotel near his restaurant, one of many popping up along the coast for surfers who have rediscovered El Salvador.

"I would do it again. No, I don't want to leave. And what would I do if I went somewhere else?

"I have faith in the town. Yes, there is some gang activity here but most tourists won't know it exists," he said, crediting the formation of a 400-member national tourism police force by the tourism ministry.

"They try extortion. They have come after me three times, and I have received threats. I don't pay them because once you do they won't leave you alone."

As a sign of the new times, the tourism ministry under the new leftist government was in 2009 headed by José Napoleón Duarte, the son of the former president of that name, whose government waged a bitter 12-year war against the left that eventually won the presidency.

Rotherham loves telling of a wartime morning when a Salvadoran military helicopter bristling with weaponry came in low over the waves right toward Punta Roca.

"He landed right on the beach there," he said, pointing to a spot maybe 50 yards away. "It was facing us, loaded with rockets, machine guns.

"The pilot came running toward us and I recognized him when he took off his helmet. He was a customer of mine. He told me he had gotten some bad food the night before and badly needed to use the bathroom.

"That was El Salvador."

Word Wars

IT WAS LATE afternoon in the sun-blasted town of Ilobasco in El Salvador's dry tobacco country, and the ultra-conservative ARENA party was ramping up for a hell-roaring 1984 presidential campaign rally.

Ancient trucks wheezed down from the rugged hills bearing farm workers to whom landowners had given a bag of tortillas and a pint of the local tanglefoot each—and a very strong suggestion that they attend.

The candidate, Roberto d'Aubuisson, a boyish-looking, rakishly handsome man who oozed charm when he wasn't having people killed, stood behind a bunting-draped podium. He was in rare form.

He held up a watermelon and a machete.

"I call the Christian Democrats the 'Watermelon Party,'" he shouted, referring to the opposing green-and-white party colors, and slammed the machete blade through the melon with a resounding *thwack*. "GREEN on the outside! RED on the inside!"

That's about as gracious as it got in the rough-and-tumble race. While terror, bullets, and shrapnel laced through El Salvador as the election neared, the word war was almost as nasty.

There were no real issues, few real arguments. Those feisty times lacked party platforms as we know them.

"I'll make it better." "You will get the piece of land you deserve." "We will stop the death squads." "We will bring peace." "We will defeat the communists."

Not likely convinced by Duarte or d'Aubuisson. Photo: Pat Hamilton.

Thus in a tiny country plagued by just about every manmade problem imaginable, and with apparently no way out, the candidates had little to talk about except each other. So they shot low and seldom missed, going on TV or climbing aboard flatbed trucks at rallies to blindly denounce each other as communists, "practicing homosexuals," liars, thieves, and more.

The social issues behind the war, runaway homicide rates and inflation, a battered economy, guerrilla sabotage, shortages of many consumer goods, corruption, civilian death squads, a military marinated in impunity, hobbled public-works projects, power outages, blown bridges, and massive wartime civilian displacement generally got short mention if any.

What nobody discussed, or really could discuss much, was how to fix these problems.

With guerrillas absent from the electoral process, there was little anybody could really do. The left couldn't win the war or the peace, but their war of attrition against the government and the economy made sure nobody else would either, and the fighting continued in varying intensity for another eight years.

The guerrillas felt, plausibly, that their candidates would be killed if they went public, and they didn't field a presidential contender that year.

Thus there was no real exchange of ideas.

In 1984 the Christian Democrat Duarte and ARENA's d'Aubuisson got the most votes in the first round and went to a runoff.

Duarte had returned in 1979 from exile in Venezuela, where he had fled after losing a shamelessly rigged election seven years earlier.

He reassumed control of the party he helped establish in El Salvador, and was finally running for the presidency his autobiography indicates he had long felt was his almost by right.

His main opponent, d'Aubuisson, a former army major and frustrated coup plotter, was closely linked to leadership of right-wing paramilitary death squads.

Parties that finished out of the money in the first round could throw their support behind either front-runner, often in exchange for a promise of, say, a cabinet post or other consideration.

Voting was mandatory but there was no other real reason to do it. The minimal fines were seldom collected.

In the 1982 election to name an assembly that would draw up another constitution, the military-backed National Conciliation Party, or PCN, which had been thrown out in the 1979 coup, bought newspaper ads in the friendly rightist press. These described Duarte (who was not yet a presidential candidate) as "pathetic, terrifying, apocalyptic, offensive, emotional, dramatic, melodramatic, exhausting, comical, waggish, festive, foolish, grotesque, ridiculous, laughable, hilarious, ribald and satirical."

Rather a lot.

To visitors the campaigns seemed a mix of puff and bluster, low comedy, lower circus, and revival meetings, all with touches of a county fair and the Wild West, worthless as news, priceless as sideshows.

"The Christian Democrats are our enemies because they are communists," bawled a d'Aubuisson warm-up speaker in the 1984 campaign in San Vicente, where the volcano looming large over the town swarmed with guerrillas.

"We have proof that the [Christian Democratic] mayor in Santa Clara meets every night at midnight with the guerrillas in his house."

A 1982 newspaper ad depicted Duarte as a vulture, waddling across a map of the country laying skull-shaped eggs.

The left flexed its muscles from the perimeter, trying to hobble the election by preventing polls from opening, burning ballot boxes, paralyzing transit, and in rare cases shooting at lines of voters.

But still the 1982 turnout was high, an in-your-face response from Salvadorans already weary of a war that would drag on for another ten years

The resulting constituent assembly gave Duarte's party a plurality, 24 seats of 60, but not the majority. The rest went to rightist parties who were hostile to him and voted as a bloc.

So Duarte sat out the next two years, waiting for the time he was sure would come, in his green cement-block party headquarters, sitting under a portrait of himself which he had painted. In fairness, it wasn't bad.

Up-country, in the war-worn northern mountain town of Chalatenango, where the light-colored hair and blue eyes are a legacy of 19th-century European coffee planters, the PCN ran a flashy campaign appealing to pre-war nostalgia of peace and public works, somehow skirting a 20-year legacy of corruption, rigged voting, and impunity.

"The candidates are coming to give us the answers to all of our problems," a warm-up speaker bellowed at the crowd, many of whom had also been trucked in from the mountain ranches. A band played a campaign song, the theme from *Star Wars*.

Fireworks burst in the air, releasing small blue parachutes.

Someone freed a box of white doves from behind the stage. The birds fluttered over the crowd, wheeling to the north toward the nearby parched hills and mountains where, probably within sight or even within sniper shot of the rally, the guerrillas were in firm control.

"The colors of our party are as blue as your eyes, as blue as the Chalatenango skies above us," shouted PCN presidential candidate Francisco José "Chachi" Guerrero.

Peasants, often shoeless and in rags, watched from the rear of the town square. Security types with submachine guns watched back through dark glasses. The Guerrero men had been in town since at least the day before to be sure their guy got in and out in one piece.

Some spectators wore colorful party T-shirts, possibly their first new clothing in ages. The shirts were infrequent away from rally sites. Wearing your politics in public could be fatal.

El Salvador could be like that.

Such campaign blitzes often were played to rural audiences, many of whom were barely literate and who had little access to information beyond what the candidates and party hacks bleated out.

So on the day of the first round of presidential balloting the names of the candidates, which many voters probably couldn't read, were not even on the ballots.

Instead there were just the party symbols, which Salvadorans had seen for weeks stenciled and plastered across everything that didn't move and some things that did, and knew them well.

Sound cars with scratchy loudspeakers prowled the streets telling people to "vote the little fish" (the Christian Democrat symbol) or "vote the cross" (ARENA) or "vote the handshake" (National Conciliation) or "vote the little arrow" (the Democratic Action Party—whose relatively moderate, likable and generally baggage-free candidate, René Fortín Magaña, somehow never gained traction).

On election day, El Salvador followed the practice of many countries, dipping each voter's finger in ink to be sure he or she didn't come back for seconds. Guerrillas had previously threatened the lives of people who had voted, so in 1984 the government came up with what they thought was a way of keeping track in a manner less obvious to the left: with a special pencil they scrawled a mark on the hand of the voter that could only be seen under an ultra-violet light supplied to all voting places.

Multiple voting was no blank issue. With massive displacement, especially of rural populations, people who moved from their home departments as war consumed or threatened their towns and villages could get new voting cards and keep the old ones.

There was no real central control.

A new computer system provided by the United States to deal with that issue found a few people with 30 or more valid voting credentials.

As the credibility abroad of the elections was a major government concern, a few foreign journalists were invited to the government electoral headquarters to see the new safeguards. A fellow journalist accepted the stripe of the waxy pencil on his hand and sat quietly next to me rubbing the mark as the conference continued. The light was flashed across his hand again. Nothing.

Out on the streets Duarte could be very good on the stump and knew how to pluck the heartstrings of a nation in which few families were untouched in some way by death, displacement, or division.

Two sons of one of the founders of El Salvador's Christian Democrats and a Duarte right hand, José Antonio Morales Ehrlich, had fought with the rebels.

During the 1984 San Salvador runoff campaign Duarte shot for the emotions.

"We must stop the spilling of blood, we must stop the tears from coming to the eyes of Salvadoran mothers," he shouted.

"We must end the days when right-wing death squads break down the doors of houses and take away husbands and sons at night."

But again, how? Nobody seemed sure.

A now-famous picture of Duarte with Guillermo Ungo, his vice-presidential candidate in the stolen 1972 election, was dusted off by rightists and shown ad nauseam to depict Duarte as a communist. Ungo later sided with a political arm of the FMLN but said he disliked what he saw as guerrilla excesses. By the 1980s he and some other like-minded politicians were in exile. Even more were dead.

Chachi Guerrero of the PCN, meanwhile, had enough votes after the first round to put either front-runner over the top if he could deliver them.* Salvadoran voters commonly followed the lead of the head of their party. So Guerrero the also-ran had clout way beyond his vote total, which may have been ten per cent.

What happened next spoke loads.

A few of us went up to Guerrero's house while this was in play to ask him what he was going to do. Chachi was a personable man, short and stocky with a wide grin, who could be a gracious host with a ready handshake. His eyes bulged somewhat.

Think back to drawings of Toad of Toad Hall from *The Wind in the Willows,* scale them back slightly, and you had him to a T. On this day he held the reins and he knew it.

---

* It was common for losing candidates to approach the front runners claiming they could deliver so many votes from here or so many votes from there, hoping to horse-trade their endorsements for some political favor or a place at the table in the new government. Most of them couldn't deliver a pizza, let alone enough votes to matter.

Chachi, with roots in the wealthy landowning class, was not of the masses. His backyard was huge—peasants farmed and lived on not much more—and covered by a net that made it into an aviary with toucans and other exotica, plus a pool.

"So, Chachi," one of us asked. "What are you going to do?"

Chachi sat on a plain wooden chair by the phone. "Nobody has called me yet," he said.

Someone eventually did. Chachi, whose National Conciliation Party had supported the military and oligarchy since he helped found it, told his backers to follow their consciences but made it clear, as he had previously, that he would rather see Duarte as president.

Duarte won and Chachi wound up on the Salvadoran Supreme Court.

Chachi was no rube. He was a former foreign minister and had helped write an earlier constitution. He was an advisor in the first of four ARENA administrations and urged ARENA president Alfredo Cristiani toward a negotiated settlement with the rebels, a position some rightists regarded as treason.

He was, it is said, investigating the 1989 murders of six Jesuit priests, their housekeeper, and her daughter, by an army patrol at the University of Central America (and may have had fresh and inconvenient evidence in the case) when he was killed. Guerrero left home with two bodyguards and was shot to death outside a hamburger stand. His killers walked up to the car and pointed machine pistols through his window.*

Meanwhile, the propaganda mills of various persuasions kept cranking out their stuff. At times government information

---

* The United Nations Truth Commission toyed briefly with the possibility that the hit was from the right, despite the fact that the left claimed responsibility for it.

campaigns were intentional parodies, and to their credit, quite good.

Nearly every morning the guerrillas' Radio Venceremos ("We Will Triumph") hit the air with a shortwave broadcast, on a frequency many Salvadorans couldn't easily get, with stirring revolutionary songs and slogans.

"Revolutionary greetings from the northern highways, the eastern mountains," it bawled, followed by a litany of rebel successes, real or otherwise.

"Mines on Guazapa, mines in Chalatenango, mines in the north of San Miguel, causing countless casualties to the forces of the dictatorship," a jubilant Radio V announcer would shout through the shortwave static. They would fight, she vowed, "until we defeat the army of apes financed and directed by American imperialism."

In 1985, near the time and frequency of the regular Radio V broadcast, an imposter station emerged, sounding at first very much like the real thing.

"Atención, mucha atención," the reader would shout.[*]

"August 19 at 7 a.m. we ambushed a troop truck...in which our military units covered the soldiers with rifle fire, which, oddly, caused no casualties.

"No doubt our fighters should work harder on their marksmanship."

The announcer would list the names of detained rebel suspects lucky enough to make it to prison alive (there weren't all that many) or trumpet and ridicule the government tally of rebel casualties.

"Our commanders are right in pressing for a third round of peace talks with the government because much of our peoples' blood is being spilled now that our sabotage of the

---

[*] In Latin America, radio's way of screaming "Extra!"

war economy produces civilian victims," the announcer of the knockoff station would claim.

Both the Salvadoran government and the Americans denied any ties to the bogus Radio V, as it was universally known. Somebody was fibbing.

There was speculation that the knockoff announcer was Inés Duarte, a favorite daughter of President Duarte, who was kidnapped by guerrillas for six hectic weeks in 1985 and who had something of a puckish sense of humor, plus experience in radio.

In the longer run Radio V, the FMLN news agency, its New York PR firm, and the government information offices had audiences beyond the Salvadoran people in mind.

Each relied more on outside than on internal support to stay in the game.

The government got billions of dollars from the United States, an amount magnified by the fact that it went to a very small place. The funding flowed despite congressmen who winced at reports of human-rights violations. The left, too, looked abroad and found willing patrons.

Unlike many other wars, the sides had no captive audience in the foreign press corps. Unusually, the same reporters covered the war from both sides. And it may have been the first time the Salvadoran government sought outside sympathy for anything it did.

The government had an efficient cadre of spokespeople willing to present their case, and it usually made top officials available. Many were young, bright, and bilingual, and those who weren't tended to be surrounded by people who were.

If you wanted another point of view, you would just drive to certain areas and hang out. "The Gs," as our embassy was fond of calling the guerrillas, would find you.

There was a stretch of deteriorating highway near the torn-up town of Suchitoto where the same clutch of Gs could usually be found.

When visiting journalists wanted to talk to guerrillas, that's where we often took them, so often, in fact, that when the rebels saw our car their reaction seemed to be, "Oh Jesus, here they come again."

There was an army outpost a mile or so away. Nobody seemed to mind. It wasn't the most violent part of the country but the fighting there could be savage.

The area around Suchitoto was controlled by the Popular Liberation Forces, which had peeled off from the old Salvadoran Communist Party years earlier and was headed then by Salvador Sánchez Cerén, whose nom de guerre was Leonel González.*

Many FPL fighters would chat at length with journalists about why they were there or how they envisioned a postwar El Salvador. Other rebel armies in the FMLN, including the key People's Revolutionary Army (ERP) in the east, could be more basic and volatile. The ERP was headed by Joaquín Villalobos, the son of prosperous San Salvador furniture dealers.

All sides had one thing in common: they lied a great deal.

That governments don't have friends but rather interests became gin-clear as the war dragged on and became known to those covering it as "the shifting sands of fact."

The United States and the Salvadorans would deny that certain massacres totaling hundreds of lives had occurred when

---

* Sánchez Cerén had been a math teacher before joining the guerrillas. By 2009 he was vice president and education minister for El Salvador. He stepped down as education minister in mid-2012 to prepare for a run for the presidency in 2014. He was the chosen candidate of the FMLN leadership, signaling in many eyes the desire of the party to steer to the left, away from the moderate policies of the noncombatant Mauricio Funes, who is term-limited at five years.

journalists had firsthand information—or even inconvenient photos—indicating that they had occurred.

In January of 1981, the government claimed to be in control of the whole country when those of us working rural areas knew that was hooey—the left controlled at least one departmental capital and had government troops tied up in three of the remaining 13 departments.

So when the American Embassy announced that the Salvadoran military had recovered boats used by Nicaragua to ferry arms to rebel forces in El Salvador it was met with a collective yawn, although there was ample reason to suspect it was so.

Nicaragua denied loudly and often that it would *ever* do such a thing.*

"This is a lie against the Nicaraguan revolution because everyone knows the position of the Nicaraguan government," huffed Miguel d'Escoto, the Hollywood-born Maryknoll priest who served as the Sandinistas' first foreign minister.

While the Sandinistas sympathized with the Salvadoran rebels, he said, that would not extend to supplying weapons or training.

Former Salvadoran rebel leader Eduardo Sancho Cienfuegos erased any remaining traces of doubt when he wrote in *El Salvador: A General History,* compiled by Óscar Martínez Peñate, that that was exactly what was going on.

The shipments, he wrote, "left Nicaragua, passed through the Gulf of Fonseca, and arrived at a [Salvadoran] beach near Tamarindo," evading sophisticated radar that had been set up in the gulf.

"These arms were picked up by the guerrillas near that beach and transported by foot to Guazapa, Chalatenango, Morazán, and Usulután," all areas of heavy rebel activity.

---

* It became common knowledge later.

The left would use Radio V to claim its forces had taken over this or that town or region. This was frequently difficult to verify since the areas often were inaccessible because of fighting or government or rebel roadblocks.

The military officials even willing to acknowledge the Radio V broadcasts usually said they were nonsense, in less polite terms.

In those days, before widespread cell-phone use in the country, most small towns had a single switchboard "central," and in many rural villages very few houses had phones. Even as late as 2009, people in small towns gave visitors instructions that might include "Go up three blocks to the telephone and turn right onto the black [paved] street."

In the 1980s a caller seeking a local resident would be told by the switchboard operator to call back at a certain time and a kid would be sent scampering off across the fields to find the intended recipient and tell him to be at the central at the appointed time.

Since the central was often the only communication in or out, the first thing the rebel or government troops would do when they moved into a town was take it over.

So verifying rebel or government claims sometimes was as simple as calling the central, if the phones were working, and seeing who answered.

Sometimes, we got lucky. In January of 1983 guerrillas hit the mountaintop coffee-growing town of Berlin, their biggest target in some time. The army rushed in reinforcements, but for reasons that escape me we couldn't get in.

So we called the mayor, José Freddy Portillo, whom one of us had met and interviewed there earlier. Never throw away a phone number.

"He can't come to the phone right now," said his wife. "He's shooting at guerrillas."

Archbishop Romero with congregation.
Photo: Archivos/Centro de la Fotografía.

Liberation Theology and the Assassination of Archbishop Romero

IN A RUSTIC rebel mountain camp tucked among small *milpas,* or cornfields, in the feisty eastern department of San Miguel, Rogelio Poncel pondered his role in the bloody mess that was El Salvador's civil war.

Poncel, then 44, was a quiet, tall man, Belgian by nationality, and a Roman Catholic priest. He roamed from camp to camp in those years to give spiritual comfort to the fighters of the People's Revolutionary Army (ERP), forces that suffered tremendous losses and hardships, forces long on determination and often short on rations.

The Vatican was pushing to get politically activist priests to pull back and re-emphasize biblical basics. The controversy involving activist "liberation theology" in El Salvador contributed to two of the more horrific massacres in the country's 12 years of civil war as church workers became targets of the right.

In late 1983 Poncel was standing his ground.

He had linked up with the rebels, he said, on Christmas Day of 1980. He stayed with them until the war ended 12 years later. In the camp above the town of Chirilagua he justified his role this way:

"The Bible confronts the established order. It must be seen from the point of view of the poor, and Christ was poor," he said in a fireside interview.

The Bible, he said, carries a message of liberation.

"A Christian, a priest, must of necessity be a revolutionary. How can we conform what we preach with a system that oppresses and exploits?"

He carried no weapon but said he knew priests with the guerrillas who did and admired them for it.

He said he knew many of the hundreds of people killed in the massacre in El Mozote and some surrounding villages by Salvadoran army troops two years earlier and had ministered to most of them.

"It made me want to pick up a gun," he said, "but the comrades told me there were lots of fighters but not very many priests."

Poncel, who was a diocesan and not constrained by a religious order, said he had received no grief from his superiors about his activities despite the change in the winds from the Vatican.

"I have a very understanding bishop," he said, and dropped the topic.

He said he had been told by rebel soldiers around El Mozote that a government sweep of the town was likely and advised residents to leave.

"But they decided to stay behind with their homes and take care of their belongings," he said.

We had stumbled for miles up rocky paths that led across stream beds and through the cover of milpas that concealed the trail up from Chirilagua after a chance meeting with rebel forces who were in the town to buy supplies.

We introduced ourselves and asked if we could go with them and they said, in essence, "sure."

Poncel sat placidly by a fire half-hidden by handwoven nets to discourage air strikes. As we talked, a couple of young women, also from Belgium, were hanging silk-screened T-shirts with rebel slogans to dry.

Down below, the rebels had dragooned several soldiers home on leave and made them carry the heavy boxes of new supplies on their backs up the steep hills toward the rebel base.

The rebel leaders were a young man and his wife who said they had been with the rebels for about four years and who spoke of their peasant roots. Their accents made them sound more like educated Salvadorans not often seen in these rustic hills, possibly from one of the universities where the rebel movement picked up steam. Their children, they said, were with friends.

The nervous soldiers, who didn't look a minute over 18, would be released in a few days, the two said, because after troops had been in rebel custody for any length of time the army considered them "contaminated" and untrustworthy. This, apparently, was not unusual.

Poncel stayed with the ERP until the peace treaty was signed and as of 2010 was based in a church in Perquín, for years the isolated headquarters area of the ERP. Today, you can go there in a tour bus.

Several other groups of priests and nuns lived in rebel territory, including some from Ohio who lived in Chirilagua and a group from Ireland in the much more conflicted town of San Francisco Gotera to the north. The Irish appreciated the drop of Irish whisky we usually took along.

Journalists, especially those resident in El Salvador, usually picked up a couple of jugs at the airport duty-free when flying back into the country and set them aside for the next trip to San Francisco Gotera.

The Irish priests usually let us stay with them and the anecdotes got better as the evening aged. They went places usually closed to us and knew the villagers in ways a casual visitor could not. They would talk freely to the extent they felt that they could without endangering themselves or violating confidences. They were evasive about their own politics and said they considered their role pastoral.

By 2009 the Irish and the groups of priests and nuns from the United States had moved on.

Others in the Catholic clergy weren't so lucky, and the church paid a terrible price for trying to defuse the war and bring the sides together, something many on the far right considered high treason.

At least 17 priests and nuns plus an American lay church worker were murdered by the military or rightist death squads.

The most widely known was Msgr. Óscar Arnulfo Romero, the archbishop of San Salvador, who dedicated much of his short tenure to urging Salvadorans not only to stop fighting but to do something about the social conditions that led to the revolution.

His murder, carried out as he celebrated Mass in a hospital chapel in March of 1980, slammed the door, if it hadn't been closed already, on any possible peaceful solution to the growing conflict.

The Roman Catholic Church in El Salvador was (and generally remains) fairly conservative, and military governments had long tried to influence the selection of the country's top cleric.

Romero, a diminutive, shy-looking man who was 60 when he assumed the archbishop's post, looked and acted like the last person in the world who would be a burr in the blanket of the military or aristocracy.

Romero took office in 1977, when discontent was beginning to increase. That year presumed rightists shot to death a Jesuit priest and close friend of Romero's, Rutilio Grande, as he headed toward a church north of the capital in the Aguilares area to celebrate Mass.

Grande was a follower of liberation theology, which had and retains a significant following in Central America. Many who knew Romero said the Rutilio Grande murder radicalized him.

Liberation theology has been described as an interpretation of Christian faith through the eyes of the poor and oppressed, giving them a "preferential option."

Many of its advocates stressed this practice over established doctrine, which riled the Vatican, including Cardinal Joseph Ratzinger, who at the time headed the Congregation for the Doctrine of the Faith.

Ratzinger (beginning in 2005, Pope Benedict XVI) felt some basic theological terms were being assigned Marxist meanings in light of current political and social situations and were being put, mistakenly in his view, in the context of class struggle. He accused the movement of trying to politically interpret the Bible.

While most of El Salvador's bishops took a more orthodox view of things, the high profile of Romero and others who embraced the liberation theology approach suggested to some that the church was a nest of subversives.

In the mid-1980s, the conservative Ratzinger condemned some elements of liberation theology and prohibited priests from teaching it.

He indicated he had no argument with helping the poor but that it should not dominate the hierarchy and traditional church beliefs.

The Vatican at the time was on fairly good terms with many authoritarian governments in the region. Predictably, the far right saw the movement as essentially Catholic communism.

Flyers and graffiti urging Salvadorans to "Be a patriot, kill a priest," began popping up by early 1980.

The church played a huge role in negotiations and human-rights issues throughout the war. It informed Salvadorans of the weekly toll of human lives lost to political murders. The numbers were sometimes iffy but reflected the scope of the horrors.

Its photo archive of death-squad victims helped families of missing relatives learn the fate of their loved ones. It brokered negotiations between the guerrillas and the government when rebels kidnapped the daughter of President José Napoleón Duarte for 44 days in 1985.

Church leaders helped organize and mediate the first public peace talks in the northern town of La Palma in 1984, which didn't end the war but provided a window of hope for the nation and a precedent for further talks.

And always, its leaders warned the country of the awful fate ahead if things didn't change, and fast.

Romero's Sunday homilies, broadcast nationwide on the church-owned radio station YSAX, were said to have the largest audiences of any broadcast in the country possibly excepting major soccer matches. A few weeks before his death a bomb destroyed the station, which had been the target of earlier attempts.

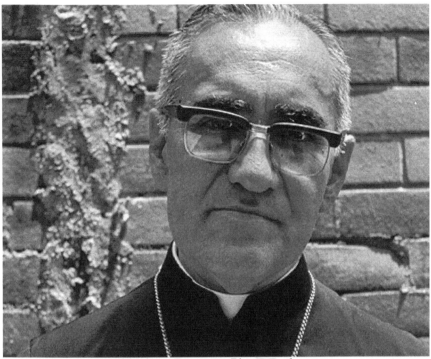
Archbishop Romero. Photo: unknown.

The bombing must have made Romero suspect his time was limited, and he ramped up efforts to stop the fighting.

In 1980 he asked President Jimmy Carter to halt military aid, saying, "It is being used to repress my people."

The capital's conservative press was attacking him as demagogic and violent, and one paper suggested that "the armed forces should begin to oil their weapons."

A week before he was killed he proclaimed that neither the ruling junta nor the Christian Democrat party ran El Salvador.

Rather, he said, power was in the hands of the armed forces. "They only know how to repress the people and defend the interests of the Salvadorian oligarchy..."

He began to go out alone so as not to endanger friends. On March 10, after he led a Mass for a slain opposition leader, a suitcase bomb containing sticks of dynamite and a faulty time fuse was found behind the pulpit.

In his March 23 homily Romero challenged government troops, who typically came from peasant ranks, to simply put down their guns and go home.

"Brothers, you are from the same people; you kill your fellow peasant. No soldier is obliged to obey an order that is contrary to the will of God…," he said. "In the name of God then, in the name of this suffering people I ask you, I beg you, I command you in the name of God: stop the repression."

The next evening, during Mass at the chapel of a cancer hospital where he had his residence, a red Volkswagen pulled up to the open chapel door and a sniper fired a single fatal shot at Romero.

The truth commission concluded that rightist leader and later presidential candidate Roberto d'Aubuisson gave the order for the assassination and that members of his security details carried it out. D'Aubuisson, who tried hard to blame it on guerrillas, was never tried. The judge assigned to the case fled for fear of his life to Costa Rica.

I interviewed Romero in his simple apartment at the hospital a few weeks before he was killed.

Vestments he apparently ironed himself were draped over chairs. Dishes he said he would get around to washing were in the sink. The typewriter he used to compose his often-feisty homilies was surrounded by loose sheets of paper at a small unpainted desk.

There was a brightly painted crucifix above the desk, in the definitive style of Salvadoran artist Fernando Llort, a style that features bright enamel vignettes of a happier countryside, gaily painted houses, improbable livestock, crops fantastical yet real. It portrayed a time that hadn't existed for years, if it ever had, and if it had, wouldn't soon be possible again. Llort always said he saw hope and incorporated that in his paintings, drawn from the idealism rooted in his earlier studies for the priesthood in Belgium.

Nothing in the archbishop's apartment gave any clue that this was the home of El Salvador's strongest moral force as the country tumbled toward wider war, a man whose death was short weeks away.

"For some time you have been cross-wise with the Vatican and been scolded by Pope John Paul II, whose dislike of liberal activist priests is no secret," I mentioned. "What about that?"

The question was a softball, but one I felt I had to ask if only so I could say I had.

His response was brief and practiced, one he seemed to feel was of almost Jeffersonian self-evidence.

How, he shrugged, could he be a man of God and not look after the welfare of the parishioners, most of whom lived in grinding poverty and virtual serfdom? If that meant taking on the oligarchy and the military, so be it.

Now, then, would I like a cup of coffee?

Gunfire broke out on the cathedral steps during his funeral. The mourners blamed the military and the military blamed the mourners. About 30 people were killed, some say more. Records are few and partisan.

That and a massacre on the same steps during a student protest in 1978 left bullet holes in the hollow iron bars that made up the fence around the cathedral. By design or oversight, some of the holes were still there in 2011.

He remains the most revered man in El Salvador, and in 2005 the Vatican opened the plodding beatification process, the first step toward sainthood. The campaign has wide but not universal support. Some more conservative Latin American clerics still say he was killed not for his faith but for his political views, a distinction Romero didn't make.

While he was alive some priests and bishops began telling the Vatican quietly that Romero was politicizing the church. His attempts to stop the killing and improve the lot of the poorest were seen as treason by many on the right.

His tomb, a much-visited shrine today, is in the basement of the cathedral, which back then was charitably described as ugly, a drab-looking concrete structure minus a finished dome because Romero had directed that money set aside to finish it be given to the poor. It has since been completed.

So some of the walls didn't quite make it to the ceiling in the 1980s, and visiting pigeons often made low bombing runs over the front-row pews full of young girls in white first-communion dresses.

At times the standing-room-only crowds in the cathedral would break out in cheers and applause as he drove home his messages.

After the assassination his successor, Msgr. Arturo Rivera y Damas, continued the message albeit in a less feisty manner.

The constitution barred priests from using the pulpit for political ends or to directly criticize the government or its officials, but there were ways.

A wall commemorating the war and Archbishop Romero. Photo: author.

During the 1984 presidential election campaign, Rivera y Damas exhorted parishioners "to avoid building their houses on sand."

The Spanish word for sand is *arena,* the acronym for the country's far-right party, which was opposing the moderate Christian Democrat Duarte for the presidency.

Asked later if the reference was coincidental, the cleric gave a coy smile and said simply, "You heard my words."

Occasionally a stand-in, the Rev. Jesús Delgado, delivered the homily. The tall, spare cleric wasn't well known to many of us although we referred to him after work and over rum as "Jesus the Thin," actually a pretty good translation of his name.

He may have laid out Romero's case as well and as forcefully as the archbishop himself did, as he rammed home his message in stem-winding homilies to enthusiastic parishioners. In the very early 1980s, groups of leftists sometimes would run through the church doors, which opened onto a busy street and plaza, and toss bundles of leftist leaflets.

The church, however, was far from a leftist monolith.

Many priests and bishops in San Salvador and in the more conservative countryside distanced themselves from the Romero message through the war and beyond. Among the country's bishops, Rivera y Damas was Romero's only solid ranking ally in the liberation theology controversy. Conservatives called him a "red bishop," and the Vatican waited three years before appointing him to replace Romero.

When Rivera y Damas died in 1994, the archbishop's miter went to a traditionalist, Msgr. Fernando Saenz Lacalle, a former military chaplain and former member of the conservative Opus Dei movement, ending two decades of politically active liberal leadership in the Salvadoran church.

It was well established by then that Pope John Paul II disfavored liberal bishops.

Central America has almost always had a cardinal, and when a spot came open Rivera y Damas, who had worked hard to end the fighting in his country, was tipped by many to be a strong contender. The job went instead to Msgr. Miguel Obando y Bravo of Nicaragua, who had suffered major indignities at the hands of the Sandinista government, which had tried to set up its own "peoples' church."

An assistant to Obando y Bravo was run naked through the streets by Sandinista thugs. At least one Nicaraguan priest was physically thrown out the front door of his own church.

The problems of the Salvadoran church leadership showed up in different and bloodier ways.

On November 19, 1989, amid a major rebel offensive (and the last major push of the war) in the capital, members of the army's Atlacatl Battalion arrived at the campus of the Jesuit-run University of Central America and killed six Jesuit professors, their housekeeper, and her teenage daughter.

The U.N. Truth Commission did extensive interviews and concluded that the orders for the massacre were made at the top levels of the military.

Ten soldiers were put on trial, two were convicted, and both were freed under the 1993 amnesty.

Saenz opposed an inquiry by the Spanish government into the killings of the Jesuits, saying it would not further conciliation efforts and that the matter should stay within the country.

Most of the slain priests were Spanish citizens, and Spain claimed some jurisdiction based on that.

After celebrating Mass in April of 2000 he proposed amnesty for Carlos Palacios and Francisco Contreras, the two National Guard soldiers still jailed for killing the American churchwomen.

"Let us have mercy and pity for them," he said. They have demonstrated their repentance.

Saenz Lacalle took mandatory retirement because of age in 2008 and was replaced by the like-minded Msgr. José Luis Escobar Alas, further cementing, if more cement were needed, the change in church emphasis.

The change was quickly obvious but became more so when Escobar Alas ordered the colorful tile façade of the Metropolitan Cathedral ripped away.

The façade of some 3,000 tiles had been the year-long work of Fernando Llort, done at the church's request.

The mural was a point of pride for many Salvadorans who have taken Llort's distinctive but much-copied style as an integral part of their heritage. The façade, titled "Harmony of My People," was one of the few places downtown where Salvadorans often took visitors. Llort said he had dedicated it to the Salvadorans baptized as "artisans of peace" by Pope John Paul II on his visit there at the height of the war in 1983.

In December 2011 Escobar Alas ordered it destroyed, and it was done quickly and quietly behind a huge curtain. The colorful tiles, representing mostly rural scenes such as the typical tile-roofed countryside cottages, a worker with his tools, flowers, and fruit, lay in a shattered pile on the ground.

Llort and his many supporters said the façade was part of the national heritage. Four months before it was destroyed the government had designated it part of the national patrimony, or heritage. The archbishop said the church never saw it that way, although the work had remained in place for 14 years.

Rev. Jesús Delgado, vicar-general of the archdiocese, contended that the tiles could come loose and harm parishioners and that the symbols did not represent the faith and were profane, thus forbidden on the church itself.

The initials "OR," for Óscar Romero, were visible on the façade, which some took as a political statement. Escobar Alas said an eye-and-pyramid symbol that had Masonic overtones was also visible.

In February 2012 he firmly rejected Llort's request to reinstall the façade.

In his "Requiem for a People's Icon" Salvadoran poet Francisco Alarcon spoke for many when he wrote that the archbishop removed the façade:

> with the brutal swiftness
> as the Taliban removed
> the giant carved Buddha

and a Rockefeller
once removed a Rivera
mural in New York.

He continued:

The mosaic mural
was too colorful, naïve,
just too folkloric

too indigenous
like the poor *campesinos*
of El Salvador

He continued that it was "too Salvadoran," too reminiscent of the war and the peace accords, that it was considered fit for a village but not the cathedral in the capital.

The hierarchy, he wrote, wants angels and archangels "like there are in Rome." He likened the trashed tiles on the ground to the thousands who disappeared during the war.

Llort, who said he was given no advance word that the mural would be destroyed, was stunned. The church had asked him to design it, he said, and he did so and installed it asking only the cost of the materials.

The destruction, he said, was "a slap in the face" to the Salvadoran and foreign artisans and artists who worked on it.

The former seminarian said he respected the church hierarchy and church desires but found the explanations for the destruction at best shaky and said the Salvadoran people deserved better ones.

"The version of the deterioration of the tiles is technically unsustainable and inconsistent," he wrote.

He might have understood, he said, if he had been asked to dismantle the façade and move what he called the most important work of his career to another location.

"I have not been able to understand why they would silently destroy a work of art of a public nature.

"I asked God to enlighten me when I designed the mural in 1997 and I have asked God to enlighten me today now that they have destroyed a work of art for no convincing reason."

Llort wrote that he hopes for a "coherent explanation" with some technical and truth-based credibility for all Salvadorans and that the church will deliver to him the shards of the tiles that can be salvaged.

"I would like to work with these tile pieces that could be salvaged to begin a work of homage that I am thinking of calling 'Dignity and Respect for the Artisans and Artists of El Salvador.'"

Mission Impossible

IN THE BLOODY FROTH of civil war, it was difficult to imagine two more different men running neck-and-neck for a country's presidency.

That the race was so close was added evidence, if more were needed, of just how polarized El Salvador had become.

The 1984 election pitted U.S.-backed moderate Duarte, a would-be peacemaker who somehow gained time for a negotiated truce with guerrilla forces, against d'Aubuisson, leader of the far-right ARENA, and, by most accounts save his own, the dark prince of the death squads that sent tens of thousands of Salvadoran dissidents and suspected leftists to their graves. His nickname, "Blowtorch Bob," was inspired by the interrogation techniques he and his minions were said to favor.

Duarte won in a runoff, but 46 percent of the vote still went to d'Aubuisson. Duarte became his country's first civilian president since 1931.[*] The last one had been displaced in a 1932 coup by his eccentric and genocidal vice president, Hernández Martínez, who ruled for the next 12 years as a dictator.[†]

---

[*] Duarte had been denied the presidency in 1972 through a fraudulent election. Duarte was leading in the vote count when the government suddenly ordered radio stations to stop broadcasting the results. Gen. Arturo Molina was named the winner the next morning.

[†] The elected civilian Duarte would finish his five-year term and hand power to his elected civilian successor in 1989, the first time that had ever happened in El Salvador.

Duarte saw long-standing social inequality and oppression as the major causes of the war. D'Aubuisson saw it more simply as a conflict fomented from abroad by communists and favored a military solution.

The United States, with its intense Cold War interest in the region, needed Duarte or someone like him to buy time to settle a stalemated war. The superpowers meanwhile kept supplying the funding and weapons as they might have done in any other country that was similarly conflicted.

El Salvador supplied the bodies.

Soon after the 1979 coup that dehorsed the country's last military president, Carlos Humberto Romero,* Duarte returned from exile to a tumultuous welcome, possibly unequaled in El Salvador.

His democratic credentials looked good, especially alongside those of a string of previous military dictators. He had paid his dues with arrest, torture, beatings, and an unceremonious deportation to next-door Guatemala from whence he flew to Venezuela and seven years of exile under the protective wing of the local Christian Democrat Party.†

Duarte may have known what lay ahead when he came back from exile. An entrenched military establishment that prospered on impunity and a riled and volatile civilian right that the military favored were hard to housebreak. While he

---

* The Romero government was oppressive and corrupt, but probably no more so than several before it, and the Salvadoran left clearly was looking at what rebels had done in Nicaragua under similar circumstances.

† El Salvador's Christian Democrats were part of a larger post–World War II movement active in Europe and Latin America meant as an alternative when many countries were toying with extremes. Duarte and others established it in El Salvador after a coup attempt from the left in 1960.

was later reviled by some for atrocities on his watch, there probably was only so much he alone could have done.

It seemed that at times he simply held his nose and did what he knew he had to do, kissing an American flag on one hand, biting what he saw as the heavy-handedness of his American benefactors on the other; pounding away against military massacres and other atrocities on one hand, denying the existence of some he must have known about on the other.

The bloody elephant in the room was the military and the security forces.

A variant of the Golden Rule says the people with the gold make the rules. In El Salvador that also applied to the people with the guns.

Duarte was drawn and sometimes quartered among the right and the military, human-rights and church organizations, a growing rebel force, international criticism, and, in a way, the American Embassy, which soon came to control purse strings and assume a major role in the conduct of a war more concerned with blocking regional leftist expansion than with the tiny country where it was being fought.

It was both a crowded and a lonely place to be.

Duarte's parents were moderately comfortable and were able partly through the help of a lucky lottery ticket to send him and his brother to Notre Dame University in Indiana, although Duarte spoke virtually no English. He studied civil engineering, graduated in 1948, returned home, married his childhood sweetheart, and joined his father-in-law's prosperous construction firm.

In his pre–Notre Dame student days he joined in movements that helped bring down Hernández Martínez in 1944 and briefly took part in a Guatemala-based exiled opposition movement.

During his exile in Venezuela he worked as a civil engineer while he awaited the call home he was sure would come. He had served three terms as a popular mayor of San Salvador in the 1960s, his first real interest in politics since returning from Notre Dame. He began preparing for his 1972 presidential bid on a coalition ticket that included his Christian Democrats. Some of his fellow candidates later sided with the left, which ARENA used nonstop against him in later years.

His protests and radio broadcasts during an uprising denouncing the 1972 vote as fraudulent got him accused of treason. International pressure, including some from the Rev. Theodore Hesburgh, the president of Notre Dame who had taken a shine to the kid from El Salvador, helped clear him and Duarte went into exile in Venezuela.

An industrial accident in Venezuela cost him three fingers on one hand, giving rise to false reports that still circulate that they had been cut off by government torturers.

Opponents and puckish friends alike would parody Duarte by holding up two fingers on one hand and saying, in a pretty good imitations of his voice, "I have told you five times…"

Duarte, who had a sense of humor in times when not much was funny, probably chuckled in private.

In March of 1980 he joined the civilian-military junta that had governed since the coup the previous October and remained until it dissolved that December. He was named provisional president.

He lost power to an ultra-conservative bloc in the new constituent assembly after a bloody brawl of a campaign in early 1982. D'Aubuisson was named head of the assembly and a conservative businessman, Álvaro Magaña, was named provisional president.

From 1982 to 1984, he spent much of his time inert in his party offices. I met him for the first time, not long after he had returned from exile, at Presidential House, an impressive, gated and columned white structure on the edge of a not-too-good neighborhood on the capital's south edge.

I had been in and out of El Salvador a lot in those times, which also were busy years elsewhere in the region, and don't recall having seen him before.

I was out scrounging around for something to write about, rarely a problem then. I dropped by Presidential House on the off-chance.

On this late afternoon the iron gate was ajar and, incredibly, there were no guards. It creaked open. The front door wasn't locked. I gave it a nudge and ventured in. Why not?

At the end of a hallway on the left a stocky man in a small office sat on packing crates and hunched over more crates he used as a desk, going over piles of papers and slowly shaking his head. One light bulb. No typewriter. No phone that I remember.

I tapped on the open door and introduced myself. He stood up and offered his hand. "José Napoleón Duarte," he said. "What do you want to know?"

We talked in vague terms about what might lie ahead for El Salvador, a little place I had come to like despite everything, and there was plenty of everything.

The underlying problems, he knew about. The solutions, not so much, and he said so.

He said he envisioned a democracy akin to the one he had hoped to head in 1972. He got one, by and large, but not for another five tough years that included the bloodiest of the war and despite bitter opposition from right and left.

The country even then was awash with murderous human rights abuses and growing military clashes. Rebel armies were formally solidifying in the hills. All these movements were but a whisper of what was to follow.

His belief in his destiny to lead the country comes out shouting in his autobiography, *Duarte: My Story* (Putnam 1986), which often assumes a smugness and self-assurance akin to that of the writing voice in Richard Nixon's *Six Crises*.

Duarte had yet to realize that the United States would be at least as powerful in El Salvador as he was. Or he may have realized it all too well. He said he learned it soon enough.

In 1984 *Playboy* published the interview quoting him complaining that Washington called the shots in the war.

In his autobiography he took it a step further saying his efforts to rein in the ambitious defense minister, Gen. Guillermo García, were stymied by rightists who had the ear of Washington.

"We tried to oust him several times but we never had enough support," Duarte wrote. "My own position as president was getting weaker and weaker because the United States started dealing directly with García. When military aid was conditioned to human-rights improvements the U.S. ambassador became more powerful than I was as president. My complaints were less important than the ambassador's because he controlled the flow of money."

He said his trip to Washington, D.C., in September of 1981 was intended to take that message to Congress. Absent an official invitation and with little power, he said, he found himself relying on television talk shows and going from office to office on Capitol Hill trying to explain his problems to anyone willing to listen. Not many were.

"My reception was cool," he wrote.

Soon after he was elected president several of us in the journalist corp got invitations for coveted one-on-one interviews with Duarte, who generally favored the shotgun approach and theatrical possibilities of large news conferences instead.

Most of us weren't aware that the rest had been called too. We dutifully trudged over.

We went in one at a time as he went over a proposal, now long-forgotten, involving something with the United States. We compared notes later.

Duarte seemed to lapse into a monotone, and the boredom and frustration seemed to rise with each repetition. Duarte could be a hell-roarer when he believed in something. Clearly this was not his idea.

"There was always a difference between what the United States thought could be done in El Salvador and the results when Washington applied its formulas," Duarte wrote.

He faced other troubles.

He faced the trauma of his daughter's 1985 kidnapping by an urban guerrilla commando in the capital. His decision to free scores of guerrillas and political prisoners to get her back cost him credibility with the military and many citizens who said the government policy of not giving in to kidnappers' demands should apply across the board, president's daughter or not.

Duarte was known to have special feelings for the kidnapped Inés Duarte, then 35, the oldest of his six children. She had run his presidential campaign a year earlier.

The rebels seized her and a friend outside a private university where Inés Duarte was studying advertising and public relations. A shootout left one bodyguard dead.

The two were held in rebel territory for 44 days while the government and the guerrillas negotiated in El Salvador and Panama for their release in exchange for more than 100 leftist prisoners, most of them wounded guerrillas, many of whom were flown to Cuba via Panama. The rebels also freed about three dozen municipal officials, some of whom had been held for months.

Julio Adolfo Rey Prendes, Duarte's friend and closest advisor, was frequently visibly shaken when he gave press briefings during the time Inés was held hostage and indicated Duarte was not weathering it well.

He said more than once that Duarte was working from home and was "very shaken but very firm."

Early negotiations were carried out by two-way radios, which the rebels insisted the government supply. We were temporarily able to monitor the talks on a commercially available shortwave receiver, a Sony ICF-2001[*], but could hear only one side of the conversations.

Competition among news outlets was fierce to the point that Rey Prendes called the AP in to ask us to propose a stand-down of coverage for fear of endangering Inés and her friend. Nearly all of us quickly agreed, both out of concern and glad for the breather.

The talks concluded in Panama after three tough days of bargaining.

The guerrillas' Radio Venceremos broadcast an interview with her done hours before she was freed in which she spoke warmly of her captors, saying she had come to see them in

---

[*] If memory serves.

a different light. The government quickly said she has been forced to make the statements and to pose smiling for photos. She also claimed later that she had been coerced and said she agreed lest her release be held up or canceled. She said had been held in a rebel camp a three-day walk from her release point.

She left the country for a time and received counseling for the so-called Stockholm Syndrome, in which abductees come to identify with their captors, much as publishing heiress Patty Hearst did in the 1960s.

Fiercely bitter over the abduction, Duarte canceled a scheduled session of peace talks with the FMLN.

Duarte also faced a hostile, mostly rightist, press. There was a steady stream of barrages against him and his government especially in *El Diario de Hoy* (*Today's Paper*), one of the two largest in the country.

The paper's lone mission, it sometimes seemed, was to savage Duarte and omit anything even vaguely positive.

Two former reporters for the paper told me years later that their standing orders were to attack the Christian Democrats as bitterly and as often as possible and to have a solid reason ready for any story that failed to do so.

Duarte would shrug his shoulders when asked about the comments. His brow would furrow slightly and he would say, indignantly, "Like any good Salvadoran I don't read *El Diario de Hoy*."

Despite his problems, the United States clearly wanted to keep Duarte in power as the only plausible alternative to d'Aubuisson and apparently ponied up some $2 million to finance his 1984 presidential campaign. Former Ambassador

White, an outspoken critic of America's role in the Salvadoran upheaval, went so far as to claim Duarte was a CIA "asset."

"We find it extremely difficult, even impossible, to work with ARENA with the reputation it has even if that reputation were not justified," an American diplomat said at the time, requesting anonymity.

White, who had said d'Aubuisson had a sick mind and called him a "pathological killer," described ARENA's advances in the 1982 constituent assembly elections "a very severe setback because these people are not modern men. They basically do not believe in democracy. They want to take the country back to where it was 20 years ago or even two years ago and that is going to create more guerrillas."

There likely was worry in Washington that a d'Aubuisson presidency might have given the radical right and the death squads a freer hand and lead Congress to leave El Salvador dangling in the wind in the face of a still-growing guerrilla threat.

Nobody knew what a military win by the left might mean, whether it would be fairly benign like the Sandinista victory in Nicaragua or something closer to the killing fields of Cambodia. Either way, the Reagan administration was determined to prevent it.

Duarte won in 1984 and the next year, in an upset that surprised even his own party, the Christian Democrats got a slim majority in the National Assembly, breaking the rightist lock on power there.

The far right remained a powerful force but its tactics mellowed.

Bruised by the loss in the presidential race and by the loss of the rightist legislative majority, ARENA voted in

1985 to remove the often-brash d'Aubuisson as leader of ARENA. They replaced him with Alfredo Cristiani, a soft-spoken sports-loving member of the landed gentry.

It was widely seen as a move to clean up the party's badly tarnished image and offload some of the bloody baggage d'Aubuisson had carried.

D'Aubuisson was named the party's honorary president for life and kept his assembly seat.

D'Aubuisson founded ARENA in 1981 to oppose the juntas, which he considered leftist or worse.

Shortly after the March 1980 murder of Msgr. Romero, d'Aubuisson made a speech saying he was pleased with the killing. Although he always denied it, there was ample evidence to indicate he had a major role in it—and in the murders of many more people he considered leftist, including the two American advisors to the agrarian reform program imposed by the junta.

He urged fellow military officers to join him in a coup against the new junta, which led to his arrest at a ranch, an arrest that also turned up weapons and incriminating documents. A prosecutor ordered his release, citing insufficient evidence, a common disposition then of cases against the military.

He resigned rather than rat out his alleged co-conspirators, said to include former President Carlos Humberto Romero, who fled to Guatemala after the 1979 coup.

D'Aubuisson or his followers were named in plans, never carried out, to assassinate Ambassador White and, later, Ambassador Thomas Pickering.

While he was avidly supported by the upper classes, his electoral strength came largely from the rural poor, who became convinced that d'Aubuisson and others like him were all that stood between them and communism.*

They were very different men. Duarte could be approachable at times; he liked to press the flesh and work the crowds. D'Aubuisson, young and boyishly handsome, rarely did so, coming across as aloof, isolated, evasive.

On what we thought was a rare interview opportunity on election day eve in the first round of the 1984 presidential vote, one of us, I don't remember who, charmed an ARENA spokesman into taking us to d'Aubuisson at an undisclosed location.

We headed toward the upscale San Benito neighborhood when our guide began taking a strangely circuitous route.

I think he sensed our curiosity. "An awful lot of communists live up there," he said through clenched teeth.

"Up there" was home to a good share of San Salvador's net worth and outside of possibly the household servants there wasn't a commie in a carload. The idea that it was a festering nest of Marxist devils was laughable but, apparently, only to us. This guy meant it.

The interview didn't happen, but our guide's attitude seemed in line with much of ARENA thought: you were either a "good Salvadoran" or a communist. And around d'Aubuisson and his followers in the early 1980s being a communist was a bad thing to be.

The FMLN's Radio Venceremos said shortly before his death from cancer in 1992 that the impending demise "seems to be an act of divine justice in this moment of national

---

* The National Conciliation Party that had governed since 1961 and fell in the 1979 coup also found its strength in rural areas, often under the eye of ORDEN and other government-backed civilian vigilante groups.

conciliation," a reference to the January 16, 1992, signing of the peace accords in Mexico City, something d'Aubuisson finally seemed more or less to have come to terms with.

His running mate in 1984, snack-food manufacturer Hugo Barerra, left the party that year to form a party of his own.

"The right needs a high degree of respect inside and out of the country. This has been our great failure and it will be hard to resolve it in the short term," Barerra said in an interview then in his factory on the eastern edge of the capital.

"We must do what we can to rectify our image and leave aside those who distort that image."

He didn't mention d'Aubuisson by name.

He didn't have to.

A boy and his wares, central public market, San Salvador.
Photo: Pat Hamilton.

The Economic War

IT WAS IN LATE 1985 that the first letters signed by President Duarte began filtering out to scores, possibly hundreds, of mayors across the United States pleading for hospital beds, wheelchairs, fire engines, and other items the country's fragile, war-worn economy could no longer provide. Buses. Garbage trucks. Anything. Please.

The FMLN saw El Salvador's wobbling economy as an opening and responded by hitting the economy harder with tactics that, absent open spigots of American aid, likely would have brought it down.

Since 1979 the rebels had burned an estimated 900 buses in a country that depended on them to get produce to markets and people to work. Direct damages to the economy in those years were estimated at $1 billion, and indirect damages were vastly higher but hard to quantify.

The U.S. Congress kept sending money, often over the objections of those appalled by the country's human-rights record.

Bridges were blasted, the electricity grid was under constant attack, transportation was paralyzed by rebel decree, and kidnappings for ransom became common.

All this and, for a time, a plausible prospect of a guerrilla victory sent hard-currency private investment that had previously found pre-war El Salvador attractive scampering abroad, usually to Miami. Unemployment and borrowing from abroad soared.

There is no record of any gushers of help as a result of Duarte's letters, but some recipients were amazed to get them. Mayor William Owens of Vienna, West Virginia, said he doubted his town could help much.

"I'll have to sit down and see what he is asking for," Owens said. "But isn't that something?"

Whether Duarte expected results from the mayors or was using the letters as a ploy to perhaps coax a little more help from Washington is not clear, but the need in those years was genuine. El Salvador's rebel siege from within had left its infrastructure battered and sagging.

"We cannot pay for what we consume with what we produce," Duarte said in a speech in November of 1985.

The drain caused by economic and military costs of the war were compounded by low global prices for some of the country's main exports, coffee and sugar.

"Taxes haven't been coming in at anywhere near the rate we had hoped," said Duarte's main advisor, Julio Adolfo Rey Prendes. This in a country where paying taxes has long been more of a suggestion than an enforced requirement, sort of like obeying the local traffic signals, as in, "If you wouldn't mind..."

In 1985 Treasury Minister Ricardo López said El Salvador had to borrow $100 million to meet public employee payrolls that year. Government workers were forbidden by law to strike but had gone years without raises or overtime in the face of soaring war-fueled cost-of-living increases.

So the 100,000 or so government employees resorted to occasional "stoppages." Not strikes, mind you, stoppages. They would show up for work, punch the clock, and do nothing.

The clerk at the post office would smile and not sell you a stamp. Calls to the state-run phone company for directory or operator assistance went unanswered. In November of 1985 about 20,000 government employees were involved in such "stoppages."

Some went virtually unnoticed, including a 12-day postal workers' stoppage in a country where home mail delivery already had been cut to once a week.

Duarte threatened tough measures but at times worried out loud that a growing confrontation with the unions could push them into the fold of the guerrillas. Many were leaning that way in any case.

The letter from Duarte to U.S. mayors referred to an estimated 400,000 Salvadorans displaced within the country, most fleeing from rural areas to the cities to avoid the fighting. The overcrowded cities were wilting under filth and piles of garbage, plus the rats and flies that go with them. Sickness traceable to sanitation problems rose at the same time. The number of displaced continued to grow.

It is fairly easy to dismiss a ten-figure hole in the mega-economy of a Western power. People do it all the time. But the economies of small nations can be extremely brittle, and more vulnerable to attempts to crush them.

In 1986, in the midst of the war, the gross domestic product for El Salvador, the whole country, was about $4.6 billion, roughly equal to the income for International Paper, No. 83 on the list of Fortune 500 companies for that same year.

International Paper did not face a full-blown guerrilla offensive and was not putting a third or so of its income into fighting a war. Between 1979 and 1982, when the violence skyrocketed, the GDP dropped by 25 percent and the estimated purchasing power of the average Salvadoran, never very high in a country with massive wealth inequality, dropped by about as much.

American aid offset some of the gap but the country could no longer meet the basic needs of its citizens. It turned to foreign and international loans.

- The government owed $88 million to foreign creditors in 1970. By 1986 this number had increased to $1.5 billion.
- From 1970 to 1979 the United States sent a total of $7 million in military, economic, and development aid to El Salvador. In 1987 it was $608 million, more than El Salvador's own entire fiscal budget for that year.
- Even with the war easing slightly, the country's economic output in 1987 was only at 80 percent of 1978 levels. Foreign aid and money sent home by family members who had left the country quickly replaced exports as the nation's top sources of vital foreign exchange.

In town after town in rural areas, the only thriving business on the town square often was an exchange house where the *remesas*, or money sent back home, was exchanged for the local currency.

Those who bought the dollars that way often used them for nonessential imports the Central Bank would not cover or, just as likely, shipped them back to bank accounts in the United States for safe-keeping.

No savvy entrepreneur would be caught dead with a bank account plump with local currency in a country where the war might continue for years, or end badly and render it virtually worthless.

As times toughened, crime increased, and by the mid-1980s private security agencies, often owned by senior military officers, were among the country's few growth industries. Their employees eventually outnumbered those of the National Police as residents sought protection from robberies by guerrillas and, increasingly, common criminals in a land now awash with weapons. This remained true into 2012.

Men, especially, often were patted down during the war years at business entrances by guards checking for weapons, and rows of numbered boxes in at least one major supermarket was supplied for those who were willing to check their weapons before entering. Some people actually did so.

Some economic challenges came from the upper classes themselves.

Under changes made following the 1979 coup, key exports were nationalized, meaning producers sold to the government and were paid in the local currency. Previously, producers were able to sell exports abroad, keeping for themselves the scarce hard currency, which was then often sent abroad for safekeeping.

Thus, under the changes, the Salvadoran government acted as exporter to recapture some of the dollars badly needed at home to import essentials and keep things, such as they were, afloat.

Officially at least, businesses seeking dollars for imports requested them through the Central Bank, which weighed their currency reserves against the perceived national need for the product to be imported. There never seemed to be enough, and an informal industry thus was born.

Economic Support Fund dollars from the United States, intended to provide essential American imports, went to the Central Bank, where businessmen would apply to buy them.

But there were other ways.

On a given day outside the main post office, waving huge wads of local currency and handheld calculators, agents trolled for the people who had received dollars from abroad, offering exchange rates far better than the government did. Buyer and seller caught one another's eye, stepped around the corner, and did the deal. No paper trail.

Back at the Central Bank there were two exchange rates. The old official rate of 2.5 colons for a dollar was available for importers who could show they were meeting a critical need.

For other purposes importers seeking dollars paid a much higher colon rate, if they could buy dollars at all, making their purchases abroad more expensive and in turn making the products too expensive for many Salvadorans.

The practice of over-invoicing became a polished art. A man with remarkably close ties to the Central Bank explained it this way in the mid-1980s:

If someone wanted to import 1,000 units of Item X at $10 each he would need $10,000 dollars from the Central Bank.

But, aha! He would invoice the items at $15 each for a total of $15,000, buy those dollars at the cheap rate, and send the rest abroad, probably to Miami, for safekeeping.

"We have both the feeling and the evidence that some of this is going on now," he said. "In addition we know that some ESF money is being used for such things as travel and low-priority imports."

A U.S. Embassy official who worked with the ESF system, which was administered by the U.S. Agency for International Development, admitted there was a problem but said computerized price lists and other controls were gradually resolving it.

Economists at the time estimated that between 1979 and 1981 alone $1.1 billion in "hot capital flight" money, almost always dollars, was sent out of the country for safe-keeping instead of being put to use to solve problems at home.

"Cold-flight" money, which might have been invested in the country but was not because of the war, was huge but harder to calculate. In 1978, a year before the war started picking up, direct foreign investment was at about $124 million. From 1980 to 1984 it dribbled in at only about $7 million a year. Companies scared by the war and bled of dollars by high-ransom kidnappings by rebels cut back or just plain went home.

The country's electrical grid was an especially tasty target for saboteurs, who went to work blasting everything from neighborhood utility power poles to the massive feeder lines that brought power down from the country's hydroelectric dams.

The French-designed grid was set up in a way that normally would make it difficult to do massive long-lasting damage, but many rebel saboteurs were disenchanted former technicians with the government electricity system and knew just what to go after, and how to do it.

When "the boys," as they were widely known, brought down a major transmission tower they often planted land mines in the wreckage to slow down repairs. The infrastructure was a sitting duck. It wasn't going anywhere.

On some mornings power poles lay like matchsticks along highways where rebel presence was strong. Power might be back in a few hours or in a few days. Some rural areas were blacked out for years.

I recall one dawn when I had been up late or arisen early, looking out of a hotel window when a motorcycle bearing two young men pulled up at a concrete power pole not 50 yards away, strapped a package to the base of it, and putted off calmly, as if headed for a cup of coffee.

Ka-whoom!

Another morning in paradise.

As the guerrilla movement solidified, kidnappings provided the income for a large part of their costs.

The Armed Forces of National Resistance (FARN), one of an alphabet soup of leftist organizations that formally combined into the FMLN at a meeting in Cuba in 1980, claimed to have culled $60 million in ransom money from kidnapping businessmen, diplomats, and others. While that figure is not readily verifiable, neither is it implausible. The guerrillas shopped for weapons on freewheeling international arms markets in Europe, South America, Israel, and the United States, all more than happy to supply anything for a price.[*]

By the mid-1980s American economic aid to the Salvadoran government was in excess of $1 million a day. In a more robust and secure economy that number would be lost in a pile of much larger figures, but for tiny El Salvador it was crucial.

Not everyone was comfortable with that.

---

[*] So if an Eastern-bloc rocket-propelled grenade or a Chinese or Soviet AK-47 assault rifle or a Belgian FAL assault rifle popped up here and there, as they tended to, it didn't always mean those countries supplied them. Much of the delivery came by boat across the Gulf of Fonseca through Cuba via Nicaragua or overland from Nicaragua through Honduras and across the almost comically porous border into rebel-controlled areas of El Salvador.

"It is worrisome to find that we depend on a million dollars a day from the United States," said Juan "Johnny" Vicente Maldonado, then the director of the National Association of Private Enterprise, the nation's most influential private enterprise group.

"We thank the American people but worry that it is establishing a dependency on our part. It is not a normal relationship between countries," he said, adding, "We know it cannot go on forever."

El Salvador had developed a reputation as a place with a strong work ethic and reliable labor force, a place that carried its weight and paid its bills. You could see it every day.

In some countries in the region, the cities gave a belly-scratching yawn as residents awakened. People showed up for work mid-morning, then took a long lunch before returning for a few hours of work in the evening.

In San Salvador at 7 a.m. the streets were filling up. The creaky iron grates in front of shops were rolled up and people were headed to rare jobs, or in search of them.

Some American aid went to trying to find new sources of income beyond the traditional exports of coffee, sugar, and cotton, which were not then providing growth. And they were vulnerable to sabotage.

On Radio Venceremos guerrillas would announce *paros,* or traffic stoppages, on highways for certain periods and make good on threats to stop and destroy vehicles, especially buses, that chose to run the risk.

Many a passenger who had jammed into the belching blue buses or climbed on the roof with everything from chickens to watermelons to coconuts was left by the side of a highway as the bus burned in front of them.

Many were privately owned and such a loss would ruin most proprietors. Drivers and passengers occasionally were shot but this was very rare. Most buses were unguarded, as a bus chaperoned by police or soldiers was considered a legitimate military target by the left.

Roads through parts of San Vicente and other sugar-growing departments often were dotted with torched sugarcane trucks with their tires shot out and their cargoes smoldering a rich, caramel-scented smoke that could be smelled several curves away.

In most of the country only a fool would drive the highways at night because of robberies, kidnappings, and worse.

You might encounter instead a government patrol, sometimes a good thing, sometimes not.

On top of it all, El Salvador, seemingly a magnet for natural disasters such as floods and volcanoes, was slammed by torrential rains and landslides in 1982 that by some figuring did more damage to the economy than even the rebels had done by that point.

The crop loss along was put at $200 million, with essentials such as corn, beans, and rice hit especially hard.

"God in 24 hours did more to us than the guerrillas did in two years," Interior Minister Manuel Isidrio López Sermeno said at the time.

To worsen matters the country was hit by a volcanic eruption and a ruinous earthquake in the 1980s.

Early on the guerrillas began realizing they would not win a traditional set-piece war and began going to small-unit sabotage efforts and hit-and-run attacks instead.

Such tactics were ideal for the war on a brittle economy, one in which they could pick what to attack and when with the element of surprise that required one good hit and a fast retreat.

The government had to guard everything against as many possibilities as it could at all times.

For the rebels it was akin to a trip through an apple orchard. The economy was the orchard. Pick this one, pick that one, then disappear.

The tactic was highlighted with aplomb the night of October 15, 1981, the second anniversary of the coup that knocked out the Romero military government.

The Puente de Oro, or Golden Bridge, was one of Latin America's longest and linked the eastern and western parts of the country along the major coastal highway, or Littoral. In a nighttime operation that apparently had been long in the planning, "the boys" reduced it to twisted scrap.

For years pieces of the once-handsome span lay in the Lempa River.

Traffic was diverted to the Cuscatlán Bridge upriver, just below the 15th of September hydroelectric dam—until New Year's Day 1984. Rebel saboteurs, apparently floating down in small boats, destroyed the bridge with plastic explosives, leading to whispers that perhaps members of the thinly stretched 3rd Brigade assigned to the area may have been making a bit too merry. Virtually every other bridge along the two roads linking the east and the west had been badly damaged or destroyed.

Traffic was detoured for the second time, now across an old railway trestle bridge, one traffic direction at a time, a white-knuckle drive over a bridge with missing railroad ties replaced by anything handy. The trestle bridge too was a frequent rebel target, but it survived.

Some smaller bridges were replaced by U.S.-supplied Bailey Bridges, Erector-Set-looking contraptions that could be put up quickly and could carry some of the traffic.

In other cases, bulldozers would cut crude roads down embankments to fording spots and drivers would take their chances driving across the rivers, a poor choice in times of high water.

Attempts were made against the 15th of September Dam and the major power lines feeding from it, sometimes blacking out parts of the country for days.

During elections, polling places in areas with no electricity closed two hours earlier and ballots often were counted by candlelight.

Being caught on the roads at night was a bad idea in the best of times, which these were not. Rebel activity and common banditry flourished. In the blacked-out areas there was little but the flicker of a candle in a home or a cooking fire in a yard.

Dark roads. Dark streets. Dark houses. Dark towns.

The Peace Treaty

THE QUEST for the 1992 peace agreement that brought El Salvador's 12-year civil war to an end lasted almost as long as the conflict itself.

In 1983 the conservative-led government of the provisional president, Álvaro Magaña, appointed a peace commission and was meeting secretly with the FMLN and that group's political arm, the Democratic Revolutionary Front (FDR), but each side apparently still thought it had a chance of winning outright without negotiating away core ideals.

Then in 1984 Duarte went public with a proposal for more talks in the mountain village of La Palma on October 15, by design or otherwise the fifth anniversary of the coup that tossed out the military government.

Expectations among the public, weary of a war that would last eight more years, soared but were not met. The sides met in the church at La Palma while thousands gathered around it as close as security would allow while leaders of the government and guerrillas met inside through the day.

There was to be no military presence by either side in the town, which the rebels often occupied at will. A good many we had seen in rebel uniforms there on earlier occasions lounged on sidewalks behind their knock-off Ray-Bans, and there was no reason to assume that the army didn't have its ringers in place as well.

But it stayed peaceful as government loudspeakers blared, brayed, and bleated praise for process from the small plaza outside the church.

Batteries of hawkers peddling souvenirs, sandwiches, and soft drinks helped turn the day into a cruelly optimistic carnival and a cold reminder that decades of division, abuse, and bitterness would not be rinsed away by a few hours of talks.

There were some minor agreements on the conduct of the war and evacuation of guerrilla prisoners, but the session didn't get near the issues of the war itself.

If anything it highlighted how huge the obstacles to peace, or even to opening serious talks, were.

The emphasis in early discussions seemed to be on curbing the violence and finding jobs for the combatants. The problems of class differences, the huge gap between rich and poor, the clashing leftist and free-market agendas of the two sides, plus the death-squad problem, remained generally untouched, certainly unresolved.

Both sides put those vital issues on hold until elections could be held out of suspicion that such differences would collapse the talks.

Professor Diana Negroponte of the Brookings Institute (the wife of John Negroponte, a veteran U.S. diplomat and ambassador in the region), faulted negotiators for not insisting on international funding to rebuild the country and train Salvadorans for a return to peaceful civilian lives.

She said a surer peace may need a new generation to dilute the bitterness of the war years.

"It takes the sons and daughters of warriors to consolidate the peace," she wrote, noting that the lack of opportunities for young Salvadorans has driven thousands into gang movements that carry on the violent ways of the past.

Guerrilla demands included a power-sharing agreement before elections and the right to keep their own armed forces after the shooting stopped. They classified the demands as non-negotiable.

Duarte, who headed the 1984 government delegation at La Palma, put his foot down hard, saying he would not negotiate power sharing but that the left was free to join the electoral process and could have any power it won at the polls. It was a position Duarte held on to, and, as it turns out, it was the way the left eventually won at the national level in 2009.

The rebels offered another round of talks in Ayagualo in November of 1985 but those fell apart when they insisted on a transitional government with their participation before elections.

The round was postponed by Duarte, some said, because of his bitterness over the kidnapping of his daughter.

The FMLN boycotted a proposed round at Sensori in September of 1986 after the government refused to pull its forces from a 650-square-kilometer area around the proposed site for the talks.

After that there were no talks until after the signing of the Central American Peace Agreement in the summer of 1987.

The agreement was reached by five Central American presidents understandably worried about regional instability. The agreement invoked the broader charms of ceasefires, free elections, democracy, and ending regional conflicts. Duarte asked the left to at least use the agreement as a framework for more talks, but key elements of his military were skeptical.

Meanwhile, the bodies kept piling up in El Salvador. Duarte ordered a military ceasefire and allowed two self-exiled FDR leaders, Rubén Zamora and Guillermo Ungo, to return if they wanted to.

In two days of talks in 1987 the sides agreed to set up two commissions, one to negotiate a ceasefire and one to address the issues of the Central American Peace Plan. A session based on that deadlocked in Caracas. They tried again in Mexico City but high-centered on a continuing rebel demand for power sharing and their own post-settlement military. The left proposed instead an end to arms shipments, an end to military recruitment, and the expulsion of military advisors, all non-starters for the government.

The United States had pretty much taken over the training of Salvadoran troops and the strategic planning of the war effort by the early 1980s. While Duarte came to resent it deeply it likely is a major reason the Salvadoran rebels did not score a military win over a moribund and often dispirited military.

The role of the advisors was kept quiet at the time but there were reports by witnesses and informers that they took part in encouraging torture and other abuses against rebels and suspect civilians.

Many military officers in El Salvador and other countries who were accused of some of the worst abuses were products of the School of the Americas, which trained them in Panama for years, and later at Fort Benning, Georgia. Training materials intended for Latin American students at the school released by the Pentagon in 1986 did indeed promote targeting civilians and the use of torture and execution, among other tactics.

As the conflict dragged out it became increasingly obvious that it had become an unwinnable war of attrition.

The left made a huge push against the capital in 1989 and captured part of it but could not hold on.

Other proposed rounds of talks had been canceled or postponed for a variety of reasons including a bomb in the offices of the leftist labor confederation and the murder of Herbert Ernesto Anaya, the head of El Salvador's non-governmental Human Rights Commission.

Neither side was reporting much progress in the talks that were being held.

So the left accepted a proposal to ask United Nations Secretary General Javier Pérez de Cuellar to begin preparing for talks.

The deal was signed on January 16, 1992, at Chapultepec Castle in Mexico City.

It disbanded the Treasury Police and National Guard, organizations blamed for many of the worst human-rights violations. The FMLN disarmed and ceased being a guerrilla group, becoming instead a legal political party. The National Police became integrated with former government and guerrilla fighters. The army agreed to cut its forces in half to about 32,000 and had done so by 1993, months ahead of schedule. It had cut the number by more than half again by 1999.

The pact also called for a truth commission to investigate war atrocities. The three-member commission piled most of the blame on rightist death squads and their military sponsors, which still riled the right 20 years later.

The deeply divided country finally opted for a negotiated settlement only when it became clear they would not get one any other way and that the foreign sponsors of both sides were quickly losing interest.

A wall with some of the names of those killed in the war. Photo: author.

How Much to Forget?

ON THE OUTSKIRTS of the battle-battered town of Cinquera, Salvadoran soldiers stopped reporters trying to pick their way through primitive back roads into the town to cover the evacuation of the remaining civilians as guerrilla forces closed in and government troops moved out.

Go back, one said. "I am a Christian and I don't want to shoot you," he added, almost apologetically.

He smiled. His eyes didn't. Nearby, the severed head, presumably of a guerrilla, bobbed gently up and down, hanging by its hair from the limb of a bush.

It was 1983 and El Salvador was still very much up for grabs in a war of attrition between tenacious FMLN fighters and a much larger American-backed government force.

Wartime human-rights outrages by both sides had become routine, leaving families and whole societies in the country twisted or broken.

One by one, as outside Cinquera, or by the hundreds, as in settlements like El Mozote and Santa Cruz Loma, Salvadorans on both sides were murdered for what they said or thought, or were believed to have said or thought. That was all it took. El Salvador could be like that.

But the conflict and its horrors have generally faded from memory in the United States, which poured billions of dollars into preventing what it saw then as the possible "fall" of Central America in the proxy conflict between the U.S. and the Soviet Union. It is becoming part of a misty past even in El Salvador itself, which saw scarcely a family emerge untouched.

Two decades after the truce many Salvadorans still debate how much the country ought to remember from those years.

The far right, which governed for 20 years beginning in 1989 through four presidential elections, wants to bury the scorching atrocities of the past, saying it is time to move on, to turn the page. Others fear that past horrors could return if they are erased from the national memory.

There is plenty to kick under the national rug. The effect of the war was overwhelming for the civilians who suffered through it, and some of the massacres almost defy belief.

A United Nations Truth Commission set up by the 1992 peace accords was given six months to investigate a dozen years of human-rights complaints, including the worst ones. It concluded that, "Bitter as the truth may prove to be in some cases, recognizing what happened in El Salvador is the first essential step in assuring that it will not happen again."

Now the country is deciding how much to tell the next generation, and how much to forget.

"It may be that some of this generation does not want to know about the war," said Msgr. Gregorio Rosa Chávez, the likable auxiliary archbishop of San Salvador, who spent years denouncing abuses and trying to nudge El Salvador toward an elusive peace. "But if we forget, there is no future." How, he asked, can El Salvadorans 'turn the page' if that page has yet to be read?"

Former political prisoners, ex-rebels, and others agree but face strong conservative opposition.

Of the thousands of submitted cases and complaints, the three-member Truth Commission picked 32 of the worst for closer study and issued its report on March 15, 1993. Five days later the rightist-controlled Salvadoran legislature approved a general amnesty covering virtually all violent events of the war and many other offenses during the war years.

Given the country's past, the future is hard to predict and while the country is stable today, it isn't known for that.

Since 1841 El Salvador has gone through some 65 presidencies and 15 constitutions, many of them short-lived "Kleenex" affairs, readily disposed of.

The presidency changed hands 14 times in the 10 years after 1841. Seven of the 12 presidents between 1935 and 1979 were tossed out in coups.

What stays in my mind is not the politicians and generals or other talking heads swelled with self-righteousness. True righteousness of any kind was a scarce commodity. My memory remains stuck on the price paid by a voiceless majority caught up in the war, by people whose only concern was seeing it end.

Records of some of the worst atrocities are somehow missing, and survivors who suffered the most or saw the worst of it say they fear a national amnesia is moving in.

The winners write the history books, and rightist administrations oversaw that task in El Salvador for two decades. Today, young eyes widen at stories of what happened just down the street or one village over, and not so long ago. The new leftist government is pledging to keep bad memories alive if only as a warning for the future—and probably also to provide fodder for future elections.

At a 2009 San Salvador reunion of correspondents who covered the war I talked with Luis Romero Pineda, a student at Central American University, where we were making several presentations to journalism students. Kids at UCA are among the brightest in the country, curious, alert, often bilingual.

Over *pupusas*, El Salvador's national equivalent of the hamburger, I asked him what we should talk to the classes about.

"Just tell us about the things you saw here, the things you covered in the 1980s, how you did it. What was it like, how were things?" he replied.

I ran a few of the worst examples past him. He fell silent and his jaw may have dropped.

"I didn't know this," he said quietly. "We have never heard these stories."

Others remember, all too well.

Just west of the capital, in Santa Tecla, former political prisoners began in 2009 to revamp the old prison where they had been held during the war and make it into a museum to preserve that point in time.

They recalled lying on the floor in the early 1980s gasping for oxygen as guards rolled tear-gas grenades in for the hell of it. Some of the walls still contain sets of four vertical lines and cross-hatches as the prisoners marked off the glacially slow weeks or months.

A weathered inaugural plaque proudly notes that it was built in 1902. The high, crenulated walls and darkened oblong gun slots still evoke a chill at first sight. It is hard to imagine anything good ever happening there.

The appearance of the place could only have added to the horror of the newly detained. It still looks like a leftover prop from a B movie.

Some of the former prisoners said they cursed their fate when they first saw the place, then thought again.

"The people who came here were the lucky ones," said Miguel Ángel Ayala, then 72. "Most of the rest, they killed."

They are grayer now, and many don't walk or see as well as they did. But on a visit during a ceremony former prisoners stressed time and again, "This is our time, it's time to tell *our* story."

Ayala, a former secondary-school math teacher, was a member of the left-leaning National Democratic Union, or UDN.

"The food was bad, we got no letters, we could not talk politics," he said. "They used to throw tear gas here at us. We used to lie on the ground to get as much oxygen as we could."

It was closed in the early 1980s with political prisoners being sent to the larger Mariona Prison, known then and now in the Salvadoran vernacular as "Miami."

Mariona now houses mostly gang members, who have replaced rebels as the country's major threat to stability.

Francisco Ramírez Abelar spent three years in the two prisons from 1981 to 1983.

"I was considered an enemy of the government," he said. His two small radio stations sometimes criticized the government line.

"They beat us while we were blindfolded. They gave us electric shocks to the genitals. They put pistols in our mouths. They threatened to kill our families if we did not cooperate with the authorities."

They were among some 200 former prisoners wearing first-name nametags and greeting each other with expansive Latino *abrazotes,* or big hugs.

"The big fight is over," Enrique Roscones, representing the city's FMLN government, told the participants.

"What we need now is small revolutions, defending what we have. Many young people do not know that there were political prisoners, that there was torture in this country. 'No, I did not know that,' they will say. This now is your part of the story. You want to be a part of that story, to repeat what happened, to be sure it never will repeat itself."

The ink was barely dry on the Truth Commission report when the Salvadoran military denounced it as "unjust, incomplete, illegal, anti-ethical, biased, and impertinent" and affirmed its "pride in having fulfilled its mission to defend our people... and our democratic republican system."

Postwar schoolbooks tend to gloss over the social roots of the war and paint the upheaval as simply a Cold War byproduct.

One textbook, aimed at seventh graders, barely touches on the car bombs, death squads, bodies in the street, massacres, repression, and terror of those years but goes on at length about the types of weapons used by both sides and the Soviet bloc origin of many of them.

The book, titled *Social and Civic Studies,* (Ediciones Servicios Educativos, 2009) says, "The war in El Salvador has been considered one of the conflicts derived from the ideological, political and military confrontations between the Soviet Union and the United States (and their respective allies) known as the Cold War."

The book stresses the role of the Armed Forces of Liberation, the largely inconsequential military wing of the country's small and now disbanded Communist Party.

Nobody reads much about Central America now, but the cycle of uprisings and revolutions, mostly in El Salvador, Guatemala, and Nicaragua, claimed upwards of 350,000 lives from 1960 to the early 1990s.

The recent book *Breaking News* is a highly readable narrative of how The Associated Press, my employer for 37 years, has covered the world since the 1840s. Even *Breaking News* devotes just a paragraph or two to the carnage and upheaval in the region over those years, despite the fact that the AP covered the region aggressively, especially beginning in the late 1970s. There is no mention at all of El Salvador, which crowded front pages for years.

In December of 1980, as the war picked up, Duarte, then the head of the country's ruling junta and its future president, was asked by Raymond Bonner of the *New York Times* why the rebels were in the hills.

His answer: "Fifty years of lies, fifty years of injustice, fifty years of frustration. This is a history of people starving to death, living in misery. For fifty years the same people had all the power, all the money, all the jobs, all the education, all the opportunities."

This wasn't new. The rebel movement had been building, in varying degrees, for many years, long before the Sandinista victory, and the problem was far from uniquely Salvadoran.

El Salvador faced stymied hopes, empty stomachs, a repressed majority, and no safety valve, a recipe for big trouble any way you slice it. The Eastern Bloc would have been foolish not to take advantage, even as democratic change was beginning to seep into the region.

The transition was not always smooth and among the Salvadoran upper classes it was unwelcome.

The tiny well-off Salvadoran minority viewed most reforms as a communist threat to the "Salvadoran way of life," which 19th-century British Prime Minister Benjamin Disraeli described in his own country as a time when life was for the few and for the very few.

You had a servant or you were one. If you were born a peasant, you died a peasant.

And the "very few" fought changes as they always had, with their own "regulators," forerunners of the modern death squads, and military cooperation to keep things as they had always been.

It was the Salvadoran way.

Salvadoran peasants aspiring to break out of class shackles often were quickly reminded of the order of things. Much of the oligarchy operated as the cattle barons of the Old West did, with murder and impunity.

As change loomed and repression worsened to contain it, unions, student political organizations, and similar groups morphed into the armed groups of the FMLN. The Front gave some order to a disparate alphabet soup of acronyms and organizations but it was far from monolithic—some components didn't get along.

Their leaders were numerous and early targets of rightist death squads who gathered behind ARENA, and its flamboyant standard-bearer, d'Aubuisson. "Bloody up to his elbows," an American Embassy spokesman once grumbled. He was being kind.

The United States meanwhile was faced with either holding its nose and continuing to bankroll its effort despite the atrocities or pulling the plug and letting the government fend for itself and possibly fall.

But through it all the horrors somehow never seemed to end. Values acquired growing up in a quiet town in Oregon were tough to apply in a tiny country at war with itself, one I couldn't have found on a map a decade earlier, one where murder was a solution to issues that seldom even cross comfortable American minds.

Most of us spent our first year or so there writing stories that tried to make sense of it. Gradually we realized it didn't make any sense and began writing about that. When we thought it couldn't get any worse, it did.

On a quiet Sunday morning in about 1981 an anonymous phone call suggested we go to a place near the capital where, it turned out, death squads had left their night's work on display. About a dozen heads were in one pile, arms in another, legs in a third and torsos in a fourth. Let the families sort them out.

And it worked both ways.

In 1985 guerrillas entered the town of Santa Cruz Loma looking for Civilian Defense Force volunteers and killed at least 20 people, including women and children. Word had to be sent to nearby towns for more coffins.

They were quickly filled. "Who's the one in the green shirt?" a worker yelled as the macabre business continued.

He was identified, placed in a coffin. The lid was quickly fastened with cross-shaped thumb-screws and loaded onto a truck. Other victims were just thrown onto the back of the truck, their legs dangling out the back as it wheezed up the rough road to the cemetery for fast burials.

The inside of one home was completely burned out except for a straw crucifix, un-singed and still fixed to one wall. I have no idea what happened to the occupants.

Other rebels executed the American crew of a helicopter they had shot down near Usulután, and killed or kidnapped at least ten small-town conservative mayors and other local officials to discourage civic participation.

These are not pleasant memories, but some fear the price of losing them could be high, maybe not soon but some day.

American advisors had been sent to transform the often-corrupt regional fiefdoms of the military into something of a cohesive unit, with standards and training bases that looked, smelled, and sounded like an American boot camp. And they succeeded. But the concept that some ideas can't be stopped with bullets never really settled in, and in the early 1980s the killings kept escalating.

The rightist reaction to the Truth Commission report amounted to diatribes and an attempt at a national hand-cleansing, à la Pontius Pilate.

Nothing really happened. Well, if it did, we didn't do it. We've lost the records. Let's not dwell on it.

In 2009 President Funes asked the country's pardon for what the government had done over 30 years even though it wasn't his government, infuriating the right. Vice president and former rebel leader Salvador Sánchez Cerén had asked for similar forgiveness for transgressions by the left.

But former ARENA president Armando Calderón Sol was not satisfied.

"The government did not cause the war," he said. "The war was caused by segments of the people, bloodthirsty guerrillas who killed and massacred."

Alfredo Cristiani, the first of the four ARENA presidents, said the report examined "only a part of everything that happened in all those years of violence" and dealt "only with certain cases and people."

This irked Sánchez Cerén, who led the Popular Liberation Forces, a key rebel army component of the FMLN, under the nom de guerre Leonel González.

The pre-war teacher became vice president and education minister in 2009. He looked a bit out of place to those of us who knew him "when," as he' sat in coat and tie behind a government desk.

"It is dangerous that our youth not know what happened in the 1960s, '70s, '80s in El Salvador," he said.

He said the textbooks published during the ARENA years present a skewed whitewash, though since that time some independent memoirs, largely by leftists, have been published outside the public education system.

"What we don't have is a discussion," about how things came to be the way they did, he said in an interview. "What really happened during El Salvador's struggle is hidden. For 20 years the government has had a policy of seeing that people do not know their true history.

"When we start talking of the truth [rightists] accuse us of being ideologically minded. The story they have been telling is their official story but we are going to begin making certain changes, we are going to begin investigating our own independence. For a people with no memory it can happen again."

"What is most important now is to see what has to be done to erase, eliminate, and forget everything in the past," Cristiani countered. "Our position is that it would be unjust to take legal or administrative measures against some but not others, simply because the latter did not figure in the cases examined in the Truth Commission's report."

He urged Salvadorans to "turn that painful page in our history and seek a better future for our country."

The Salvadoran Supreme Court also attacked the Truth Commission report, which had accused the court of obstruction of justice and of tolerance of impunity in some major cases involving massacres

The Inter-American Human Rights Commission seethed at the amnesty, calling it more of an impunity measure, and urged its repeal. But Funes sided with his rightist predecessors and others who argued against "opening wounds" of the past and said he would not seek its repeal.

The Inter-American Human Rights Commission contended that El Salvador is obligated to try to prevent rights violations, punish those responsible, and compensate victims adequately.

The rights commission is also fond of the Vienna Convention on the Law of Treaties, which says a nation cannot unilaterally use domestic law to duck legal obligations imposed by international treaty.

High-profile cases included the previously mentioned 1981 massacre at El Mozote and nearby villages, in which troops of the American-trained Atlacatl Battalion, among others, wiped out hundreds of residents.

There were the 1989 murders, also by the Atlacatl, of six Jesuit priests, their housekeeper, and her teenage daughter at the University of Central America and the 1980 murders of three American nuns and a lay Catholic social worker. Much of the worst of the rest was pushed into relative obscurity by the scope of high-profile incidents, and most of those happened in or near isolated rural villages far from public view.

The Truth Commission also received more than 800 complaints of violence in violation of international law against the FMLN, including the murders of local mayors and other noncombatants.

But in its methodical, almost mechanical ferocity, the El Mozote massacre at least rivaled that carried out by American troops in My Lai, South Vietnam.

The commission said that despite easily available evidence Salvadoran officials did not order an investigation and even denied that it had taken place, as did the U.S. Embassy, initially.

Detailed forensic investigations did not begin until 1992. The commission concluded that more than 200 residents of the village, at least half of them children, were systematically murdered in groups.

Investigators said the toll may have been higher because bodies of some victims, especially small children, were incinerated when troops burned buildings. Other body parts were mixed and fragmented from the impact of close-range machine-gun bullets.

Top-level Salvadoran military officials contended there were no records for that period, thus no information was available.

The Truth Commission report said the president of the Salvadoran Supreme Court, Mauricio Gutiérrez Castro, interfered with 1990 judicial proceedings involving the massacre.

In the summer of 1992 he visited the exhumation site and said the examinations proved that only dead guerrillas were buried there.

The government declined to move against those believed responsible, saying they were protected by the 1993 amnesty. So survivors and family members of victims took the case to Inter-American Court of Human Rights, which operates in conjunction with the Organization of American States. In December 2012 the court ruled that the killings took place "within the framework of a systematic plan of repression to which certain sectors of the populace were subjected during an internal armed conflict...." That "armed conflict" ended with the 1992 peace accords and the establishment of a Truth Commission—whose recommendations both sides promised to accept.

President Funes had apologized the the victims' families the previous January. After the court ruling, the government, through its foreign ministry, said it recognized the court ruling and its own responsibility. The foreign ministry statement accepting responsibility for the massacre said the orders of the court would be honored.

The 2012 court ruling said that the victims and families were entitled to compensation ranging from $10,000 to $35,000.

The court ruling noted that the Truth Commission called for punishment for those responsible, for reparations to victims and family members because the case extended to human rights violations, and that the government was obliged to continue the investigation until an adequate conclusion is reached.

The court further said the use of the amnesty law to suppress the investigation violated "the letter and the spirit" of the peace accords and seriously affected the obligation of the country to probe and punish human rights violations.

Remains of 281 victims had been confirmed, the court noted, but that the number of dead was likely in the 1,000 range. It ordered a number of measures including a better census of the victims and guarantees that the amnesty law would not be used to impede the investigation. (Many of those likely to be held responsible have died.)

The Atalcatl was the first of several specially trained rapid deployment infantry battalions used in the war and the one with the worst abuse record.

The Truth Commission also concluded that in May of 1980 the army, National Guard, and members of ORDEN shot down at least 300 noncombatants who were trying to cross the

Sumpul River to Honduras to escape a military sweep of the northern department of Chalatenango.

The massacre got heavy coverage in the news media in Honduras, which, despite its then-military government, had one of the more unfettered presses in the region. A formal complaint was filed by the priests and nuns of the Honduran diocese of Santa Rosa de Copán that June based on interviews and witness reports. It accused Honduras of complicity.

Salvadoran defense officials denied the massacre had taken place. The Truth Commission said it was told by Salvadorian authorities that there were no records for that period. Duarte later admitted there had been fatalities but said all were communist guerrillas. In fact, many were children.

In March of 1981, after a military operation in the rebel stronghold of the department of Morazán, Army Capt. Carlos Napoleon Medina Garay ordered the deaths of the civilian population of the village of El Junquillo, about 60 in all, ranging from an 80-year-old man to a day-old child. Soldiers and civil-defense forces also raped girls under the age of 12. Despite public complaints at the time there was no investigation.

In September of 1988 Salvadoran army troops arrived in San Sebastián in the department of San Vicente, where Lt. Manuel Jesús de Gálvez was told four men were involved in subversive activities. One who was detained showed troops where weapons and explosives were hidden and implicated others.

The lieutenant was ordered to "eliminate" the detainee but refused without first having orders in writing and offered to hand over command of the unit.

De Gálvez followed orders to detain six more suspects. Maj. Mauracio de Beltrán Granados ordered the ten taken to a place where an ambush could be faked. Troops were told to finish off any survivors. Only one soldier, Manuel de Jesús Herrera Rivera, refused to obey the order to kill the survivors. Peasants in the area told human-rights workers and journalists that the peasants had been murdered. President Duarte publicly denied that. Only Maj. Beltrán Granados was charged, and he was shielded by the amnesty.

In April of 1989, special operations units of the Salvadoran Air Force attacked an FMLN mobile hospital and killed a French nurse, an Argentine doctor, and three other civilians. In September of 1990, a Spanish physician working with the FMLN, Dr. Begoña García Arandigoyen, 24, was killed by army troops in the usually quiet department of Santa Ana. A Salvadoran autopsy concluded the shots were fired from a distance. One done in Spain found powder burns indicating they were fired from inches away.

In August 1982 at El Calabozo army troops, again from the Atlacatl, killed over 200 captive men, women, and children. The victims were fleeing a major army sweep of an area where rebel activity was heavy. Witness reports said most were machine-gunned. Two weeks later Defense Minister José Guillermo García said an investigation had shown no massacre had taken place and later told the Truth Commission that there were no records for that period. The commission said it could find no evidence of any investigation.

As discussed in a previous chapters, on March 24, 1980, the archbishop of San Salvador, Msgr. Óscar Arnulfo Romero, was shot to death while celebrating Mass in the chapel of a cancer hospital.

The commission cited overwhelming evidence that d'Aubuisson ordered the shooting carried out by members of his own security force and said the Salvadoran Supreme Court obstructed the investigation. There was never a conviction.

In November of 1989, as has been recounted previously, an army night patrol entered the University of Central America campus and shot to death Jesuit priests including the rector who taught there plus their housekeeper and her teenage daughter.

It happened during the administration of President Alfredo Cristiani, who was president when the amnesty was passed.

The Salvadoran Supreme Court later ruled that crimes committed during the Cristiani presidency, the last three years of the war, were exempt from the amnesty because a government still in power cannot pardon itself.

The list goes on.

While many of the incidents took place in isolated areas, thousands of the victims are commemorated today in a very public place.

In Cuscatlán Park near the center of San Salvador a high wall of gray Spanish granite maybe 100 yards long or more, paid for by private donors, contains the engraved names of civilian war victims, some 30,000 and counting, a reminder of another wall in Washington D.C.

There is a special section for children who were killed and an acknowledgement that the names of untold thousands of victims will likely never appear. Kids today kick soccer balls and frolic in the shade by the wall with cotton candy or mangos on sticks and look up only once in awhile at the grim gray engravings.

The wall and park are across the street from the military hospital where in 1979 troops on the roof sometimes would open fire with automatic weapons on funeral marchers taking dead suspected leftists to a cemetery. Days later the coffins of those marchers would be carried down the same street, sometimes with similar results.

Those of us watching all this dove into recessed doorways and prayed to the sweet Baby Jesus. As the gunfire died down, taxis summoned by friends swooped in to pick up the victims. Afternoon rains rinsed away the blood. There was plenty to wash away in El Salvador.

El Salvador Today

TWO ROAD TRIPS from Oregon back to El Salvador nearly 20 years after the peace treaty still found me confronting reflections of its turbulent past, at least in part because of gang problems almost as deadly as the war they replaced.

Gang violence has boosted the per-capita civilian murder rate to the second-highest in the world after neighboring Honduras. Most murders go uninvestigated and only about four percent of the nation's homicides result in convictions.

Probable gang-related homicides had reached 4,300 for the first 11 months of 2011. About 2,000 more Salvadorans went missing in that time, many presumed to have been gang casualties.

The 2011 murder rate was pegged at about 71 per 100,000 people, compared to about 4.8 per 100,000 in the United States and 6.9 globally.

In 2012 Gen. David Murgía Payés, the minister of justice and security, said about 90 percent of the murders were gang-related.

"People who do not believe this is a war of gangs don't live in this country," he told the respected online newspaper *El Faro*. "This will not improve in our country with the collapsed judicial system we have here in El Salvador. We capture about 220 people a day [for various crimes] and there is no legal system here now that can process that great a number of delinquents each day."

In the 1980s death squads often left their gruesome handiwork in public places for all to see. Today's visitors here for beach or business might never know of the gang problem if they didn't or couldn't read the paper.

Most victims are poor, male, aged 15–35, and unlikely to be widely missed by anyone beyond fellow gang members or immediate family if they have any. It is all much less obvious than a shooting war.

Most things are.

But signs of war were everywhere in the 1980s.

I moved to El Salvador from Costa Rica in 1984 and soon got used to dawn breaking with the rapid *whump-whump-whump* of Huey army helicopters lifting off from the Estado Mayor, the Salvadoran Pentagon, for their morning rounds, flying low over our house and the heavy hollow crunch of bombardments by A-37 jets on suspected rebel targets just a few miles away.

Soon might follow the *clump, clump, clump* of combat boots jogging down our street and the cadenced chant, "Guerrillero, escúchame, te mataré, te mataré" ("Guerrilla, listen to me, I will kill you, I will kill you...") two, three, four, until it faded out of earshot.

And then the bus would pull up to take my 11-year-old son Chris to school.

In the evening the Hueys came back, and huge flocks of green squawking parrots flew across the capital to the now-quiet volcano, El Picacho, that looms over the city. Strangely we never saws the parrots leave from there during the morning.

The neighborhood was more secure than most. Some American Embassy officials lived there, as did the Marines assigned to protect the embassy, plus a number of Salvadoran wealthy worthies who vanished behind the high walls around their homes at night. I never did see who lived in some of the houses, and broken glass and razor wire along the tops of the walls discouraged curiosity. So did the guys with guns at the entrances.

It's a picture of serenity today. But in 1989, after we were back in the States for a time, we saw television news footage of running battles on and around what looked a lot like our street and our house, as government planes bombed parts of the city thought to be in rebel hands.

The offensive served only to convince both sides that after a dozen years this was a war nobody ever would win, so a serious move toward peace talks began.

The guerrilla war is long over but El Salvador has not been able to collar gang activity, which began to rise in the 1980s.

In those years the United States made it relatively easy for Salvadorans to immigrate if they could show a likelihood of political persecution, and tens of thousands headed north, often to Los Angeles, where they ran into established Mexican gangs.

Those who couldn't get visas went "wet," as they said, often answering any of dozens of ads in the morning papers offering to get them through Guatemala and Mexico and illegally into the United States, and even to escort them to any private address they named.

Intimidated by Mexican gangs, Salvadorans formed their own for defense, and when they ran afoul of the law, as many did, they were deported, bringing the gang tradition home with them. They usually arrived broke, jobless, and rootless, with families, if any, shattered and scattered by the war.

Many had only each other. A lawless culture settled in and by 2012 many younger entrants into Salvadoran gang life were third-generation.

Many got by with small-time drug deals and shakedowns until the expanding Mexican cartels raised the ante as they found Central America fertile ground for smuggling routes.

There is vastly more money in play today, and even now bus owners or drivers, shopkeepers, and others are killed for opposing gang demands, as are some gang members suspected of wavering loyalties.

Transport companies in 2009 estimated that about a quarter of their income went to pay extortion demands or "protection."

El Salvador has tried, with some success, to isolate visitors from all of this.

A substantial force of federal tourism police has been sprinkled around popular visitors' destinations to keep tourism, an increasingly important part of the economy, growing. In 2009 El Salvador held its first fair for foreign tour operators and drew representatives from more than 20 countries.

"The object was to mark El Salvador as a tourism point, to put out a competitive product and capture a market that was new to us," said José Napoleón Duarte Duran, the son of the former president who had fought the FMLN tooth and claw. The younger Duarte was named tourism minister in the FMLN cabinet, which says a lot about changing attitudes.

"Our campaign is to build confidence that the problems of the war that ended in 1992 are no longer an issue."

Overall the country seems one where you can find trouble if you seek it, but if you avoid some areas, don't do stupid things, and don't get crosswise with certain interests, trouble probably will not come looking for you.

While the United States and others fret over expanded influence of drug cartels, the homicide rate, at least, seems to be largely an internal issue of gangs versus gangs, not yet worthy of the hugs and affections of the superpowers that characterized the rough-and-tumble 1980s.

Both sides have mellowed since the war, and in peacetime neither extreme has yet turned out as bad as it once promised it would be.

Some differences and changes are hidden by partisan sniping and partisan deals among multiple parties with changing alliances. Others are way easier to spot if you look at the place today and remember "la época," as many Salvadorans call the bad years.

Head an hour or less south out of the capital to El Puerto del Diablo, or the Devil's Door, a mountain park with a sweeping view, a quick and refreshing get-away from hot and hectic San Salvador. Families picnic there today.

In the early 1980s, as described earlier, it was one of a number of dumping grounds for victims of rightist death squads, where bodies were chucked over the high, sometimes foggy cliffs down to the outskirts of Panchimalco for people like Armando Paz to find. Today, Panchimalco, a heavily indigenous town of cobbled streets, is known more for aspiring art galleries than for its grisly past.

People used to avoid the park for fear of accidentally seeing something they shouldn't. The park's biggest problem today seems to be a small corps of determined free-lance evangelicals slow to comprehend polite disinterest.

Across the valley and the town a narrow, almost too-picturesque highway winds through the hills toward the coast among groves of coconut palms, mango trees, sugar cane, and villages of simple whitewashed stucco homes with red tile roofs, the stuff of postcards.

A solo drive beckons a stop for a time to soak in what appears to be the old El Salvador and its rustic tranquility. I made the turn and headed up into the curves.

But here too all was not what it seemed.

When I told Luis Romero, the longtime resident AP photographer, of the pleasant detour to the coast in 2011 I could almost see the blood drain from his face.

"You did what? Pendejo! Next time ask us first."

The night before, a half-dozen people had been found hacked to death along the road, probably victims of gang rivalries. It seems the road was known for it.

But things like that now seldom are reported outside the country.

Since the 1992 peace pact and the collapse of the Soviet Union, El Salvador slipped off the radar as Washington no longer had much to oppose.

El Salvador had gone, quite unwillingly, from decades of being an insular coffee and banana republic to a world focal point.

As suddenly, it reverted to the relative backwater it always had been.

For journalists El Salvador was a choice assignment in its day, but by the mid-1990s most of the news organizations that had poured millions of dollars and huge staffs into covering it had packed up and headed for juicier stories or for home.

The old wheeze at the time was "If it bleeds, it leads," acknowledging that blood and gore in horse-doctor doses had way too much to do with what went onto the evening news or, I'm sorry, into a lot of print stories.

Editing desks, especially those of TV networks, in distant New York demanded "bang-bang," as it became known: close-up stuff of combat. We did try to shoehorn in some of the reasons for the bang-bang.

By the mid-1990s El Salvador had stopped bleeding in ways that held world attention.

The American Embassy had moved from a close-in vulnerable building, one prone to the occasional rebel rocket-propelled grenade, to a new walled villa-like structure near the city's edge, built when the duration and outcome of the conflict still were in question.

It may be a disservice to call it a diplomatic backwater today, but it no longer attracts the diplomatic powerhouses like ambassadors Dean Hinton and Thomas Pickering that it did in the Reagan years, when the line was drawn over leftist expansion and the outcome remained a crap-shoot.

The political extremes have reined in their homicidal excesses and govern together mostly as spirited adversaries rather than sworn enemies.

Most diplomats today would consider the FMLN-dominated government center-left, a long walk from what many of the rebel leaders were preaching during the war.

The whole region has changed.

When I arrived in Central America in 1979 every country there except Costa Rica was a military dictatorship. Today all are democracies in one form or another.

Some made the change fairly quietly. Honduras had a military government for two decades but quietly agreed to elected civilian power in 1981. The military governments were generally benign as military governments go; the country had one of the freer presses in the region and was by and large a country of small farmers and landowners. People could let off at least some steam if they wanted to, within reason.

Grayer heads may still recall a political cartoon in a student newspaper depicting Gen. Policarpo Paz García, the last military president, escaping partially dressed out the back window of a burning house of easy virtue. Beyond a probable snotty phone call from the presidencia there were no repercussions that I ever discovered.

The relative tolerance of the Honduran military governments and the influence of the U.S. presence, which used the country as a base for the "contra" war it waged against the Sandinistas in next-door Nicaragua, kept Honduras from the flames.

True, there were abuses and at least one rather noisy death-squad scandal, plus a nascent rebel movement, the Cinchoneros, who were active for a short time mostly in the 1980s, but they posed no real threat and were more of a nuisance. They did hijack a couple of passenger jets and pulled off a rather spectacular hostage-taking of many of the nation's wealthiest business leaders in San Pedro Sula.

One of my favorite memories of Honduras, and they are few, followed some in-house discontent over the country's pro-American stance. Military officers grabbed Gen. Gustavo Adolfo Álvarez Martínez, the head of the military, and gracelessly dumped him on a plane to neutral Costa Rica on the correct assumption that the Costa Ricans would let him in (or almost anyone else) at least for a while.

The harumphing and indignant Álvarez called a news conference in a high-end hotel overlooking San José and appeared dripping with gold necklaces, rings, bracelets, and, if memory serves, a gold Rolex.

One of us had the bad manners to ask how he managed all that on a Honduran military salary.

The unfortunate general looked us square in the eyes and said, "My wife is very frugal in the kitchen."

True story.

Against all advice he eventually returned to Honduras, claimed to have found Jesus, and was assassinated.

The transition was similar in Guatemala where a brutal war largely centered on indigenous peoples of the highlands during a long string of military dictatorships took an estimated 250,000 lives, some say more, over 36 years ending in 1996.

The military government and its economy were circling 'round the drain in many ways, and the military seemed to be saying that if it went down the tubes it wouldn't be on their watch and threw the place open to civilian elections.

Nicaragua was a whole 'nother story. Tens of thousands died in the Sandinista revolution that in 1979 toppled dictator Anastasio Somoza, the last of a dynasty that enjoyed American support for decades. Thousands more died in the U.S.-backed contra revolution in the 1980s, which tried to oust the Sandinistas, who appeared deeply ensconced enough by 2012 to be able to hang on to power one way or another as long as they like.

Panama began to bubble after populist Omar Torrijos, who took power in a 1968 coup, was killed in the poorly explained crash of his small plane in 1981, paving the way for a series of short-lived presidencies.

These ended when Gen. Manuel Antonio Noriega, a Torrijos protégé and CIA asset, took power as de facto leader in 1983. He stayed until a 1989 American invasion chased him from power—all the way to an American prison after a (dubious, some say) drug-trafficking conviction.

We later farmed him off to the French who had money-laundering issues with him, and he returned to Panama in

2012 where multiple charges awaited him. I have seen the insides of a few Panamanian prisons, not as an inmate. He may well have been happier in France.

I digress.

Only Costa Rica avoided the storm.

It was a social and political laboratory of sorts but other countries in the region spent little time learning there. More's the pity.

Over the centuries it had avoided the "cacique" system of a few large landowners and an oppressed peasant class, having been largely settled by European farmers who tended to work their own land. There was little known mineral wealth for the Spanish to plunder.

It abolished its standing army after a 1948 revolution and has long been neutral in regional disputes, which have been many. Opposing political and rebel groups in the region openly had offices there in the 1980s, sometimes only blocks apart, and political parties usually swapped power every presidential term or so with parades, bands, banners, and a minimum of fuss or recrimination.

It has a small legal Communist Party everyone knows about, and its candidates pile up a small but predictable number of votes each time. In other countries in the region military governments might have come after them. But here the party was known and was tolerated like any other. No big deal. They joined in the campaign parades along with the big boys and passed out cloth hats with red ribbons bearing the hammer and sickle. I still have one somewhere. (The party was also legal in Honduras, but would have been required to turn over its membership list. Nobody was quite that dumb.)

Latin American countries say they "celebrate" their elections even if they are violent messes. Costa Ricans actually do.

Nobody picked on the place—it somehow wasn't considered polite. Occasionally I asked government officials what would happen with their neutrality in a crisis as much of the region smoked and crackled around them. Universally I was told that the country had total faith in a 1947 treaty that said an aggression against one signatory was an aggression against all and that "all" would come to the defense.

I think the treaty, signed in Brazil, is still gathering dust somewhere. I know of no time when it was ever invoked, although there were times in the region when it well might have been.

Instead of guns most Costa Rican police in those years carried screwdrivers to remove license plates of improperly parked cars.

As my wife at the time found out, it often worked this way:

She was whistled over for an infraction of some sort, and the officer who waddled up to her car said, "In Costa Rica you can't do that! Well, you can but you shouldn't," and waved her on.

Linda liked to say that Costa Rica was "cute," but she did it a disfavor. It merely did many things right.

It was that kind of place. In El Salvador and Honduras the poorest lived in indescribable hovels, often devoid of all but disease and hunger. In Costa Rica a near-middle-class home likely had electricity, running water, often a TV, and maybe a car in the garage. Even the poorest were vastly better off.

There were exceptions of course, but generally schools and health care were good and there was upward mobility. And generally a country with those things in that region in those years did not erupt in armed rebellion. Costa Rica tried, even when it couldn't afford it, to give people what they wanted.

During a state visit to Costa Rica by President Kennedy, Costa Rica realized it did not own a cannon to fire the traditional salute. The story is that it had to borrow one from nearby Panama.

I know of no better example than Costa Rica to highlight the differences in the region.

More changes are visible.

For decades, especially before the end of the war, the doings of the Salvadoran police were a dark, secret, and feared affair, and in most minds, horrible.

Today the police force issues online press releases detailing the arrests of murder suspects, gang members, and others who earlier might have vanished without a trace.

In the past, you might have heard the plaintive plea of a parent: "Has anybody seen my son (Antonio, Luis, Federico), last seen wearing dark pants and a blue shirt, he was a shopkeeper and had no enemies…"

Panamanian celebrity Rubén Blades, singer, actor, Harvard grad, and one-time presidential candidate, wrapped up the Salvadoran situation at the time in a particularly haunting song called "The Disappeared." I still shudder when I hear it.

In March of 2012, El Salvador held elections for a national assembly and all 262 city halls, the first national referendum on the FMLN government since it took power three years earlier. ARENA campaigners stressed increased security and toughness on crime as gang violence soared. The FMLN stressed more jobs, but unemployment still was in the 38–40 percent range.

ARENA won 33 of the 84 seats, one more than it won in 2009, but was recovering from a nasty dissident movement in which 12 deputies had defected to a new party. The FMLN lost four seats to wind up with 31.

Thus neither could dominate the assembly without the help of smaller parties, and how they might vote on a given issue was uncertain. It is whispered (loudly) that many of the "swing" voters are for sale.

And though losers may still bawl for stake and stove-wood as they commonly holler "fraud," and exchange often-plausible accusations of ballot-box stuffing, coercion, and worse, the process and the society seem vastly more open under the new order.

El Salvador votes for president again in 2014. President Funes, who appears to be more popular than his party, cannot seek a second term.

For decades the element of election-night suspense was comically absent.

From 1915 to 1927 the four winning presidential candidates, snug in the hug of the military, ran unopposed. Things opened up a bit in 1931 when Arturo Araujo beat four other candidates, but he was quickly tossed out in a coup led by his vice president, Maximiliano Hernández Martínez, who unleashed a reign of terror against the left and went on to run unopposed three times. Results weren't even posted for his last win.

In 1945 the winner gathered an amazing 99.7 percent of the vote in a six-man race. Bringing up the rear, poor fish, was José Cipriano Castro, with an official total of one vote. Maybe his mother loved him.

Throughout the war San Salvador remained a droopy, often dingy, and crowded Latin American capital. Pickups full of nervous soldiers cruised the city nonstop, stubby rifle barrels pointed out the cab windows. There was always, always one sitting with his legs dangling off the back of the pickup bed, alert to an attack from the rear as the rebels gradually moved aspects of the war from the countryside into the capital.

Today parking police no longer pack submachine guns and rebel graffiti has long since faded from most stucco walls.

People are no longer patted down when entering banks, and the supermarket near where we lived has retired its rows of pigeon-hole boxes where shoppers were asked to deposit their pistols before entering.

Consumer goods were limited during the war years and many store shelves were sparsely stocked. Imported luxury goods, for the few who could buy them, were scarce, often controlled and probably bought with black-market dollars.

In the 1990s El Salvador gradually retired its official currency, the colon, and now uses American dollars.

Today modern shopping malls are thick with specialty stores full of high-end imports and buyers. It remains a poor country but clearly more people have money and are spending it instead of shipping it to Miami banks.

Reminders of the old and the new El Salvador are side-by-side. A street in one of the capital's better neighborhoods is named after a Communist rebel leader and leads to the trendy Pink Zone where restaurants and nightclubs go full-bore into the small hours.

But many recall the Pink Zone on a June evening in 1985 when a pickup full of urban guerrillas drew up alongside an outdoor restaurant and opened fire, killing four off-duty Marine guards from the American Embassy and several others.

Some things haven't changed. Clusters of the very poor still huddle in tin and cardboard shacks in the barrancas, that crisscross the capital through San Salvador's wealthier neighborhoods.

Early each day barranca dwellers like the kid with the green mango still appear over the lip of the gullies headed to jobs or more likely in search of them, dressed in spotless white shirts or blouses.

The informal economy, where people get along buying and selling what they can, was always there but has exploded to out-of-control levels, choking off even some major streets. Everyone seems to be selling. Who's buying is less obvious.

Mangoes, lengths of cloth, coconut candy, pirated CDs and DVDs by the thousands, melons, cheap clothing, open-air tables of un-refrigerated meat and seafood, small plastic bags of water said to be clean, vegetables, quack medicines, baskets of limes, balls of twine, envelopes of salt, cigarettes, used electronics, used parts that might fit your car or not, used books, cases of sodas, and live iguanas are all hawked by vendors strong of lung, perhaps a sunnier version of what a street market in Charles Dickens's London may have looked, smelled, and sounded.*

---

* In October 2012, the city government bulldozed away 33 blocks of the streert vendors' stalls saying it wanted to clean up the downtown and in essence gentrify it. This was done in a surprise nighttime operation. But since the nature of these things is that they tend to reestablish themselves, it might be a temporary development.

Kids still wander down the center strips of main streets holding up trussed, sad-eyed armadillos by their tails, critters prized locally as a soup ingredient.

We used to buy them for a dollar or two after minimal bargaining, drive them to the outskirts of the city, cut the twine that bound their little paws, and set them loose with the pointless admonition to not get caught again.

They made a rustling sound in the back seat, so we named them Russell I, Russell II, and so on. I have no idea how many Russells we sprung over the years. Quite a few. The anthropomorphist in me wants to think they looked back and murmured "thanks" as they waddled off.

We learned later that Russells often carried leprosy, which, along with cholera, was one of a handful of illnesses I ducked over the years. Typhoid, malaria, dengue, and hepatitis were another matter, and they laid others in my craft low as well. Among the less fortunate Salvadorans they remain major killers.

So do the gangs.

Offshoots of the two largest gangs, Barrio 18 (also known as the Mara 18 or the 18th Streeters) and the often-nastier Salvatrucha 13, are cropping up in some American cities, or at the very least, gangs here are adopting the names to enhance their own reputations.

Christian Poveda, a talented video producer and cameraman, spent many months gaining the confidence of the Mara 18 in the tattered suburbs of San Salvador and put together a brilliant documentary, *La Vida Loca*, or *The Wild Life*, about the gang culture.

Then in 2009 someone walked up to his parked car and shot him four times in the head for reasons not entirely clear. In 2011 ten members of the Mara 18 and a policeman were convicted in the killing and sentenced to terms of up to 30 years. The arrests and convictions themselves signal a change in the country.

The documentary was not supposed to have been released in El Salvador but pirated copies quickly found their way to the open-air markets of the capital and speculation was high that some of Poveda's killers didn't like the way they and fellow gang members were portrayed.

That was all it took. While some things change, others do not.

ARENA governments beginning in 2004 employed a tactic called *mano dura* (firm hand) against the gangs that included house-to-house sweeps by police and soldiers, but judges often refused to issue warrants for such searches.

The courts eventually ended the program and a stronger follow-up called "super mano dura" replaced it. A 2011 Freedom House report said unofficial vigilante death squads with possible police or army ties were emerging to do the job themselves, uncomfortable reminders of the death squads of the 1980s.

In 2010 the government outlawed gang membership, a move that had limited effect. Newer gang members simply stopped getting tattoos, making it harder for police to identify them.

The supply of candidates for gang membership grew. By 2010 nearly half of the 18,700 or so gang members deported back to El Salvador from the United States had criminal records. Many wound up in prisons designed to house a third of the actual number living in them, and the gang culture further intensified there. A high poverty rate, even by local standards, made gang life attractive to many young poor Salvadorans.

Estimates of gang membership numbers in the country run to 20,000.

Meanwhile the United Nations Working Group on Arbitrary Detention visited the country in early 2010, concerned that government anti-gang tactics were overriding basic freedoms.

It was one of many problems President Funes inherited in 2009, along with a $500 million budget deficit from 20 years of ARENA government, a huge amount for such a tiny country.

A 2010 World Bank report found some $200 million in discretionary aid funds received during the administration of President Tony Saca, the last ARENA president, to be somehow missing. Saca was kicked out of the party and formed a breakaway party of his own.

Hard-line leftists in the FMLN began distancing themselves from Funes, claiming he had become too moderate, even borderline rightist.

This aside, the country is open for business again. Tourism is on the rise, and the country today is thick with banks and ATMs that spit out dollars, not colons.

Among other things the change in currency to the dollar makes it easier to control inflation, because the government can no longer simply "roll the printing presses" when it needs more money.

The downside is that in giving up its own currency the country cannot easily adjust exchange rates to affect imports or exports.

Gradually, manufacturing and processing are taking the place of a dominant agricultural economy, easing pressure on a limited amount of farmland for a growing population, a factor that fomented the war.

Places once off limits to most Salvadorans are open again.

El Salvador Today

The highway to La Palma, a delightful artisans' town high in the piney-wood mountains a few miles from the Honduran border, once was a twisty, potholed affair involving roadblocks and checkpoints set by one side or the other. You planned on four to five hours and maybe didn't get through at all.

The army and the Popular Liberation Forces seemed to trade the town back and forth without much fighting, although the rebel forces seemed to be using it almost as a rest center on our several visits there.

There is something deliciously calm now about the place, and its reputation as an engine of the country's handicraft industry brings waves of tourists.

It was the site for the first publicly announced peace talks in October of 1984. We visited the town to write a "setup" piece a few days before the talks. Armed rebels strolled the streets as if they had nothing better to do.

A confident young guerrilla looked down a hillside, watching, we supposed, for some sign of government activity.

"Los bichos [the insects] are afraid to come fight us," he said. "You gringos gave them everything but guts."

Today there is a luxury inn nearby. You can rent horses.

It's the same way in Perquín, in the northeastern department of Morazán, a town that was the headquarters of some guerrilla operations for years and was difficult or impossible to get to.

Today you can go in an excursion bus, and wounded former guerrillas will, for a modest fee, guide you through the rebuilt offices of the old Radio Venceremos studio or through the FMLN museum (which consists largely of photos and captured weapons, plus the scraps of a couple of downed government helicopters, of which they remain fiercely proud).

As we drove the twisty road into the town in 2009 during a reunion of correspondents there was a sign advertising a paintball range in an area where once the shots had been fatal.

Another sign at the head of a road heading into the hills featured some blurred words and, in clear letters, the word "MINED," which sounded like an invitation to stay the hell off of it, even if it was in English.

A closer look revealed that MINED was the Spanish acronym for the Ministry of Education, which was building a school there.

Generally the country has had a fairly smooth slide from the war years to two decades of rightist presidencies to national and local governments run by the former guerrillas and their now-milder FMLN.

Perhaps no place is a better example than Suchitoto, a lakeside town that is again taking its place as a low-key resort getaway an hour or so from the capital.

As the war crackled around it one day in 1985, townspeople gathered to honor the town's patrol saint, Santa Lucía. And many who had fled the fighting returned for the occasion.

The local beauty queen rode on a small tank through the cobbled streets in army fatigues, a yellow sash, and high heels, followed by a parade of little girls in white crowns and dresses going to first communion. As soldiers marched by skyrockets burst overhead and barefoot kids waved at a departing army helicopter. The door gunner waved back.

The guerrillas still held the ragged volcano, Guazapa, that looms above the town. At times they had the town hemmed in against the lake.

On one visit we got past the army checkpoint and into town without much incident and arranged a talk with the garrison commander, who wanted to know if we had encountered any "subversivos."

We truthfully said we had not and he made it very clear he thought we were lying and probably were rebel sympathizers. The tone was chilly.

We were a mile or less out of town on the way back when photographer Jeff Robbins poked me in the ribs and pointed to several men with bits of red and black ribbons (indicating the FMLN) tied to the sights of M-16s that were leveled at us.

We told them who we were and continued without further incident, but we understood the hairy eyeball we had gotten from the garrison commander. The woods were full of them.

When the war picked up in 1980 Suchitoto had some 35,000 residents. About 6,000 remained in 1985.

Guerrillas tried to take it for years. Thousands of residents fled to the capital or elsewhere, anywhere. But the upheavals were even worse in the 32 rural *cantones* (villages) that surrounded the town and were administered by it.

Some rural residents moved into abandoned houses in Suchitoto. Guerrilla *masas*, or civilian support groups, moved into houses abandoned in the cantones, and by 1985 little regional real estate seemed to be in the hands of its rightful owners.

Guerrilla forces controlled road access for years and would not let government crews do maintenance. The lush countryside slowly began reclaiming parts of the highway. Shells of houses gave way further to weather and vines. The hospital was a charred ruin and local gasoline was a fond memory.

"The people had to get water from the lake," said Alejandro Coto, a civic booster who tried to persuade people not to flee, in 1985. "We all knew where the good springs were but when we would go to get water the rebels would shoot at us." The phones, he said, were a joke "and every time a butterfly goes by the electricity goes off."

During the war many Salvadorans waxed nostalgic about the lakeside getaway, its colonial inns and buildings, its clean, quiet cobbled side streets, the *clop clop* of animals pulling delivery carts, the cool evening calm, the lakeside park. There was little not to like. Here, as everywhere, the war changed things.

In 1983 guerrillas attacked a bus leaving Suchitoto for the capital and justified the act by saying there were soldiers guarding it (there were) thus making it, they claimed, a legitimate military target.

Several of us were headed there with an American fact-finding mission that included the late peace advocate and folk singer Mary Travers (of Peter, Paul and Mary), who became a strong opponent of American support for the Salvadoran government.

Mission organizers knew the area was no tea party and assigned one mission delegate to each of us who had some patina. I got Travers.

If it hit the fan, they were told, "stay with your journalist." I'm not sure to this day why we were the anointed guardians, but there it was.

On the floor of the smoking bus, halfway into a ditch, lay the brain of a young girl. Once in town we came across her family, who had her in a plain wooden coffin covered with a sheet. They said she had left for the capital to try to enroll in school. She was 16. "Do you want to see?" the father asked, beginning to remove the sheet. Travers, who had shown boundless curiosity on the trip, did not.

Suchitoto was among the first cities to elect an FMLN government after the 1992 truce legalized that party and the town began evolving back to its better self.

By 2009 it was again a sparkling colonial gem. The military barracks was a hotel, the white church glistened almost blindingly in the sun, the streets were clean, and several inns were doing apparent good business. At the lakeside park boatmen offered rides on canopied passenger launches that recalled rural resorts from the 1920s or 1930s.

On an October morning a crowd of priests, police, town worthies, doctors, nurses, and bystanders gathered on the swept, cobbled town square as hundreds of gallons of local moonshine confiscated in recent raids was dumped, with some ceremony, from jugs and barrels into a public sewer.

Some had been repackaged as the legal tanglefoot—Tic Tac, Troika, and other fine brands—but smelled just as bad as the real stuff did as it gurgled down to join the even lesser fluids of the town sewer.

The very affordable homemade product sometimes was served up in a concoction known as *cochebomba* (car bomb). It had recently left ten imbibers dead.

(During the war years, when rural conditions made things tight, we found it was possible to drink the legal stuff by adding water of a green coconut, ice, and plenty of lime juice. At times we got down lagoons of it, but never if there was anything else. A Vietnam buddy in north Alabama recently gave me a taste of a local artisan effort marketed there as "Wildcat." It was vastly superior.)

Suchitoto's FMLN mayor, Javier Martínez, whose nom de guerre was Walter Funes and who still answered to it, was in his second term then. But for 12 years he had been a guerrilla commander up on Guazapa, a base for rebel activity in and around the capital, surviving at least a dozen major government offensives.

He was elected by more than 70 percent of the vote each time and said he sees the early FMLN victories in local elections mostly as a laboratory that paved the rebel road to the presidency in 2009.

The party picked a new candidate for mayor in 2012, who also won. Martínez was named to a higher post.

In his modest office just off the plaza Martínez said there were early mistakes but, "We made our advances locally. Suchitoto was among the first ten towns where we won power and we still have it."

He said as he saw it, the party had the five years of President Mauricio Funes's term to get things turned around or face a serious challenge from defeated rightists or others who would promise to somehow unscramble the Salvadoran egg.

"I believe many people feared the FMLN at first. Then the people came to realize we weren't going to burn their children and turn their ashes into soap, but that we had programs that will help their pocketbooks. It was a big jump for us as a party."

He said the new government then supported six health workers and three midwives in nearby rural communities. "That's not a lot, but before, we didn't have any," he said. "We never had government help for health care. It all came from [non-governmental organizations] or the church."

He said the city was buying school uniforms, shoes, and school supplies to each pupil. "They used to call it free education, but it wasn't free," he said. "If we can make the uniforms here it will give jobs to people here and they can keep the money. It will have an impact on the local economy.

"We are guaranteeing seed and fertilizer for half-hectares [about 1.25 acres] of land. That's enough to grow corn for a year to feed a family of five," he said, adding that the plan is expanding as money allows.

"Call it populism if you want but our goal is to eliminate extreme hunger and poverty. We think families should not starve for lack of seed and fertilizer."

He said the United States among others has helped by renegotiating debt.

For the 20 years it was in power, he said, ARENA concentrated its efforts on its own party and within the government.

"They no longer have that base to work from. The FMLN isn't making that mistake. We're putting our efforts in the countryside."

He said he got involved in the rebel movement as a teenager and stayed through the 1992 signing of the peace accord.

He recalled the United Nations' Operation Paloma (Dove), which tried to advance sputtering peace talks while he was with the rebels. "We left here in UN helicopters for Toncontin Airport [in neighboring Honduras] and went from there by UN plane to Mexico," he said. "I was a part of that. We didn't get the informal ceasefire we wanted but it was important to talk to the military officers. We came back and rejoined the fight."

When it was over, he said, the rightists erroneously assumed the FMLN would demobilize politically as well as militarily.

Ricardo Galeleo Aregueta Flamenco, whose war name was Joel Sánchez Bonilla, was wounded and hustled to Cuba for treatment and also returned to rejoin the fight.

He was a member of the Armed Forces of Liberation, or FAL, the military wing of the country's small now-defunct Communist Party, and was then in charge of keeping thought lines kosher among the troops on Guazapa.

Aregueta Flamenco, who was 58 in 2009, bears nasty scars from bullet and shrapnel wounds to his elbow and chest after stumbling into a night ambush in 1985. He still can't move some fingers. "I lost three pieces of bone here in my elbow," he said. "They sent me to Cuba [for medical care] via Nicaragua—that was the route—and I came back to rejoin the fight."

During the war he occasionally sneaked into town from the volcano to see his family.

He said rebel casualties were horrendous but expressed no regrets. "It was worth it. We made our gains. We took ARENA out of the government and that was the most important thing.

"I do not believe this will happen again here. Our problem now is common crime," he said, referring to gang activity.

"We are looking to a better future. It could not be worse than our past."

Linda

DEATH WAS A PART of daily life in Central America in the 1980s, and it hit us all in different ways. Most of us lost friends and colleagues. Many of us were just numbed by the quantity of it, some of us had our lives immeasurably scarred and changed by it. Both were true of myself.

My scar came on the night of May 30, 1984. I was in Managua working on some economic stories, returning to my hotel from dinner.

We were living then in Costa Rica. My wife of 17 years, Linda, a former high-school English teacher, was a reporter on that country's very good English-language weekly, the *Tico Times*.

She had gone where I too might have been, a jungle press conference just over the Nicaraguan border on the San Juan River with former Sandinista commander Eden Pastora. He was a leader of a splinter group of the contra movement dedicated to defeating the leftist Sandinistas who had taken over in Nicaragua five years earlier. A lot of people didn't like Pastora and wanted him dead.

The Sandinistas saw him as an enemy, but not their biggest threat. The United States viewed his splinter contra force as divisive. There were rumblings, never proved, of drug dealing.

At the hotel desk the clerk took me aside and said, in effect, "Sr. Frazier, there has been a bad explosion on the San Juan. You need to knows this."

Nobody knew or would say more. Information was scarce, and dubious in Nicaragua in those years.

I think I recall my mouth going dry and that a dizziness set in as I wandered up to my room, I remember it was No. 411, and sat. Where could I call? Who might know? What could I do?

I knew Linda was with Pastora. We had a code meant to end-run the often tapped phones calls, and I had talked to our son that day.

"Momma has gone to see the man with only one oar in the water," he had said. Many thought Pastora had moments of instability.

Rumors began flying, of course. I recall walking down to the CBS offices, where I had many friends, and they knew about what I did but were calling in every favor they had to learn more.

I was able to get a couple of calls out to Costa Rica to friends who said they had heard the same report. No more.

I finally was able to get a Costa Rican station on my portable radio, where there was a live remote broadcast from the San Juan. The reporter was describing the scene as the canoes that had taken the journalists to the conference came back with victims of a large bomb that had been planted in the rude shack where the conference was held at a jungle clearing called La Penca, a ham-handed attempt on Pastora's life.

He described the victims as best he could, including a red-haired woman, probably a foreigner, "who now is without life."

I knew. I denied it but I knew.

I desperately phoned our bureau chief, the late Eloy Aguilar, in Mexico City. All he could bring himself to say was, "Joe, Joe, it's true."

Of the rest of that night I remember little. I knew I had to fly back down to San José in the morning and tell our ten-year-old son, who had been staying with neighbors overnight.

What would I say? How could I say it? I remember hobbling on crutches (from an unrelated injury) across the tarmac at Managua's airport to the TAN-SAHSA plane for Costa Rica in a light rain and a half-dawn. I remember being met in San José by the *Tico Times* editor, Dery Dyer. I remember walking up the long airport stairwell to the top, where Linda usually awaited my returns from what then were frequent and long news trips in the region.

At home the people who had cared for our son, Chris, had kept him out of school but hadn't told him why. Several Costa Ricans also were injured or killed in the bombing and the city was abuzz with it.

I sat down, called him over and said, "Chris I have to tell you something and it isn't going to be easy."

He looked at me and said, "Mommy died, didn't she."

I don't know how he knew but he had heard fellow journalists tell enough stories over his few years that he knew what it could he like "out there" in the turbulent 1980s, be it in El Salvador, Nicaragua, Guatemala—places we headed, especially when it got ugly.

From then on I don't remember much. The AP worked wonders in its support, sending in people to help, to run interference, to make arrangements I don't think I could have made, and made it clear that all I had to do was ask for more if I needed it.

The phone began to ring. "How sorry we are..." A few people stopped by although we lived well into the countryside. Co-workers from the country and the region began to arrive.

The next two or three months were, and pretty much remain, a blur. I don't know for sure where I went, to whom I talked, what I did. I know I went to our corporate headquarters in New York City, where Linda and I had planned to see the Broadway musical *Cats* on our next home leave. The AP had two tickets, good ones, waiting for Chris and me.

I remember a doctor's appointment in New York, I think, where I was told I needed a hernia repair and had for some time. I do remember getting that done in my hometown of Eugene, Oregon, but don't remember much more. I recall a nurse in the recovery room who looked at my chart and said, "Costa Rica? Did you know that woman who..."

I explained and she walked away in tears. I don't know who felt worse.

The haze lifted gradually. I recall returning to Costa Rica to pack up the house for a transfer to El Salvador, which is where I spent most of my time anyway. The Costa Rica job was constant travel, now no longer a possibility for a single parent.

I remember the anger, bitterness, and confusion that continued for years. I wanted to hit someone, or worse. But who?

I blamed the CIA for some time, as did others, because they were capable of such a thing and because they were among those who wanted Pastora out of the way of the greater contra effort it sponsored against the Sandinistas. As it turned out, a *Miami Herald* investigation led by a close friend, Juan Tamayo, determined that it was the Sandinistas themselves who ordered up and carried out the bombing with no apparent concern for the innocent people who would become victims.

It was in El Salvador, I guess, a place whose horrors already were familiar enough, that some perspective from the scraps of what happened began to settle in.

The people I saw on the street or talked to daily in cities and in the turbulent countryside there, risked this trauma every day, and thousands became sopped in the sorrows so common to the region.

In some way I guess I had become one of them. That helped. But not much.

Linda and I had known each other for 20 years, since our days at the University of Oregon.

In El Salvador I intensified my acquaintance with a field producer from CBS News, Carla Farrell. We were married two years later, and we have a son of our own. Chris is established in a successful career. Our son Jamie is doing well in college. Lives do come back together.

But it still hurts. I suppose it always will.

Joe Frazier retired from The Associated Press in 2009 and now lives in Portland, Oregon with his wife Carla.

Please contact Joe with feedback, questions, and requests for interviews, through his publisher:

>Joe Frazier
>c/o Karina Library Press
>P.O. Box 35
>Ojai, California 93024
>frazier@karinalibrary.com

Please consider leaving a review, which will help others discover the book:

elsalvadorcouldbelikethat.com/review

Made in the USA
San Bernardino, CA
19 December 2013